Woman's Guide to Money Freedom

Saving, Investing and Building Wealth for Beginners

JOSETTE MANDELA

Woman's Guide to Money Freedom

This book was originally published as Money is Freedom: A lifelong plan for achieving economic independence.

First published by Brindled Butterfly Investments Inc
1015 Atlantic Blvd, Suite 402
Atlantic Beach FL 32233

ISBN: 978-1-7348771-1-3 paperback
ISBN: 978-1-7348771-6-8 ebook
Library of Congress Control Number: 2025903615

DEDICATION

I wish to dedicate this book to my dad, whose love and support helped me become the woman I am today.

This book is also dedicated to all the women who feel overwhelmed by financial topics. For all the women who were told:

- Women can't do math
- Managing money is a man's job
- Don't worry honey I'll take care of the finances and you take care of the house and kids.

This book is for you.

I believe in you.

FREE BONUS MATERIAL

Go to https://www.josettemandela.com/freegift4u
and download your bonus material.

PART ONE

The Workbook

"Success is not final, failure is not fatal: it is the courage to continue that counts."

- Winston S Churchill

While the financial principles presented in this book are universally applicable, they are particularly crucial for women. This book is written from a woman's perspective for women, addressing the financial challenges many women face. It is not that these techniques are unique to women or that only women can benefit from this book.

Unfortunately, financial inequality remains a pressing issue. Far too many women find themselves living in poverty or financially dependent on their partners. Many women lament that their husband/partner controls the finances leaving them in the dark about their assets, important documents or even basic bill payments. This lack of financial knowledge can have serious consequences should something happen to their husband/partner.

This book is meant for any woman who feels overwhelmed by financial topics.This book is designed to show women that managing money is not hard. It is something you can do even if you never graduated from high school! To put it simply, if you can read this book and follow the simple suggestions within, you too can become financially independent.

I know some of you are saying, "My husband doles out the money and tells me what I can do with it."

There are others saying, "I am on welfare with two kids and I can barely pay for food."

Yet *others* are saying, "I never graduated high school. I don't know anything about money or banks and I'm afraid I will lose everything if I try something new."

Still others are saying, "I make a decent living however, it seems like every time I get a few bucks in my savings account, an emergency comes along and I am back at ground zero again."

My promise to you is that by the time you get halfway through this book, you will discover a way to start saving toward your financial freedom, no matter your current circumstance.

You'll never look at your life or money the same way again.

CHAPTER ONE

IN THE BEGINNING

"Don't be pushed around by the fears in your mind. Be led by the dreams in your heart."

—Roy T. Bennett, The Light in the Heart

There are no materials necessary for this exercise. The only requirement is a comfortable place to meditate and an uninterrupted 5-10 minutes. Maybe sitting in a chair, lying in your bed before you go to sleep at night, maybe sitting in a cross legged position on the floor.

For those who have never meditated before, meditation is the act of quieting the mind and focusing your attention.It can take many forms: a mindfulness practice, guided meditation, transcendental meditation, to name a few. For the purpose of this exercise, we will be doing a mindfulness practice.

Preparing for Meditation

In the beginning, your mind will rebel. It has been running your life for a long time and doesn't want to turn off. It thinks it has to be constantly vigilant, always looking for danger. To help your mind accept that meditation is a safe activity, you can set an alarm, if possible use a soft chime as the sound, so your mind knows there is a time limit.

To get into a meditative state, find a comfortable space where you can sit undisturbed for the duration of your practice. Create an inviting environment by dimming the lights, adjusting the temperature and eliminating distractions.

Choose a chair, preferably one with a high back that supports your head and neck. If you would prefer lying down or sitting on the floor with your back against the wall, that also works.

If you are in a safe place then gently close your eyes. If you do not feel safe closing your eyes then look at a spot 3-4 feet (or for my non-US audience about 1 meter) in front of you with soft, unfocused eyes.

Entering a Meditative State

Start by taking a few deep breaths - inhaling through your nose and exhaling slowly through your mouth. Allow your breath to settle into a natural rhythm. Now, let your mind wander. Do not focus on anything in particular. This exercise is designed to connect you with your inner guidance, subconscious mind, spirit guides, revealing insights that may be hidden from your conscious awareness.

You may find that soft music (no vocals) or saying 'OM' to yourself helps you get into the flow. I recommend music with no vocals as the words can prevent you from reaching a contemplative state.

Start with five minutes per day. You may find that starting each day with this mindfulness practice sets you up for a more productive day.

By meditating regularly you will find you have access to a deeper understanding and become more focused and less distracted. With the added benefit of being more resilient.

I have learned that understanding what to do does not always translate into actually doing the things consistently. That is why we are starting with mindfulness. Being aware of your predominant thoughts surrounding money can help you see what is useful and what is old programming that is no longer serving you.

Maybe you grew up believing that being rich makes you a target or that rich people are not trustworthy or that money is evil. These are quite common stereotypes. The reality is you don't have to be rich to be a target of a scam. Most crimes are random, being in the wrong place at the wrong time, clicking on a malicious link in an email or on a website.

As for rich people not being trustworthy, if you watch the news you see rich people going to jail for being untrustworthy, however, there are many more that are just living their lives without being in the headlines. The news sensationalizes everything to get you to watch. You need to be more discerning with what you choose to feed your brain. That is what your mindfulness practice can help you with.

The concept of money being evil has been corrupted. The actual quote from the bible is the love of money is the root of all evil.

These are just a few of the money myths that may be holding you back from financial freedom.

That is why you need to start your financial freedom journey by working on your inner game.

By spending quality time with yourself, your spirit guides, your God, or whatever entity you call on in times of stress, you can more quickly integrate the material in this book.

I would like you to commit to 5 minutes per day where you are simply quiet, doing nothing while listening to what the universe has to say about your financial future. You can use this time to ask the universe for guidance on what needs to change and feel into what it is like to be wealthy, to have a financial plan that feels spacious and fun rather than constricted.

With your mind tuned into the possibilities, you will be in a better state to learn and retain the money skills necessary to turn your current financial overwhelm into financial abundance.

SUMMARY

In this chapter you learned:

- Meditation is an important skill to keep you on track and engaged with learning about managing money.
- Minimum practice is 5 minutes per day.

CHAPTER TWO

GETTING STARTED

"I'm a success today because I had a friend who believed in me and I didn't have the heart to let him down."

- **Abraham Lincoln**

Materials Required:

- Small notebook. Make sure it will fit in a purse or pocket and can be carried everywhere.
- Pencil or pen.

Welcome to the first day of the rest of your financial life. Today, we are going to get started on your journey toward true financial freedom.

Though you may not realize it, this book will transform your financial situation and lead to a more confident and happier you.

To get started on your financial journey, you're going to need a small notepad and a pen or pencil to write with. Though some of you may be tempted to use your cellphone as a tracking tool, I find it easier to see the patterns when the information is on paper.

The purpose of this exercise is to capture money movement, both income and outflows. If you don't know where your money is going, it is going to be hard to create a budget, manage and grow your money and ultimately, to reach financial independence.

Over the next two months, every time you pay a bill or receive any money, write it in the notebook. Income includes everything. That's right. Paychecks, money found on the street, and even birthday gift money! Bills include rent, utilities, car payments, Starbucks coffee purchases—if you spend money on it, you should write it down.

You need to list everything you personally spend money on as well as any money you receive in order to get an accurate view of what's happening with your finances each month.

An example of what your notepad entries might look like:

Date	Time	Spent	On What
Jan 1	12pm	$1500.00	Rent
Jan 2	7am	5.50	Starbucks coffee
Jan 5	3pm	1200.00	Bi-weekly paycheck
Jan 5	6pm	250.00	Groceries
Jan 6	12pm	0.25	Found on sidewalk
Jan 6	6pm	10.75	Dry cleaning
Jan 12	7am	200.00	Electric bill
Jan 15	7am	55.00	Cell Phone bill
Jan 19	3pm	1200.00	Bi-weekly paycheck

At this point, I do not want you to change anything you normally do. Just record every penny spent, as well as every penny earned over the next two months.

At the end of two months, we will review all entries and look for patterns. When we do, you're going to want some blank paper and some highlighters to help split out the income from the expenses.

SUMMARY

In this chapter, you have learned:

- A system for tracking your money.
- Do this daily.

CHAPTER THREE

TWO MONTHS LATER

"Success is the progressive realization
of a worthy goal or ideal."

—**Earl Nightingale**

Materials Required:

- 6 #10 business size envelopes or equivalent or 6 clear plastic containers
- 1 Black magic marker
- 30 uninterrupted minutes in a quiet location

Note: If you already have a bank account, then you don't have to create envelopes for all the categories listed here. However, I strongly recommend even those with bank accounts create a *FUN* envelope as that is money that you will spend monthly. For those with bank accounts, creating subaccounts for each of the envelopes helps you segregate the money and make it clear what each account is for. Only create sub accounts, if there is no cost associated with doing it.

You have already read Chapters One and Two and completed the exercises. You are reading this book and hopefully have decided to give it a chance.

At this point, it's likely thinking about a budget makes your head hurt. That's why your action plan for today is simply getting acquainted with the basics of money management.

To keep our discussion of money management simple, we are going to separate the money outflows into 6 categories. These categories are: Necessities, Long-term savings, Entertainment (Fun), Charitable contributions, Ongoing education, and Retirement/Financial Freedom.

We will start by labeling envelopes or plastic jars with the black magic marker as listed below.

Necessities (Must have)	(NEC–55%)
Long-Term Savings for Spending	(LTSS–10%)
Fun	(FUN–10%)
Charity/Giving	(GIVE–5%)
Education	(ED–10%)
Retirement/Financial Freedom	(RET–10%)

Stop and do the exercise now

The percentages listed on the envelopes are your long-term goal. You only want to spend at most 55 percent of your income on necessities, such as food and shelter. For today, I will assume you are living like I was many years ago—paycheck-to-paycheck. Any emergency that required an immediate cash outlay, no matter how small, was enough to cause panic.

If you have trouble with percentages, don't despair. I will explain more about how to divide up the money using the above percentages in the next chapter

For today we will focus on 2 envelopes, FUN and RET. For some of you, an envelope labeled FUN must look like a cruel joke. I can practically hear you asking, "How can I have FUN with circumstances like this?"

Though I may not have been *exactly* where you are, I do understand your skepticism. However, it's important to not let your doubts get in the way of reaching financial freedom.

Even though the goal is to put the proper percentage of money in all 6 envelopes, it's unlikely that you're already in a position to do that. You need to start somewhere, and this is a place to start.

What we are working on creating is a lifelong process for reaching your goals.

Notice RET and FUN state 10 percent. This means that when you are financially able to devote just 55 percent of your current income on necessities, then RET and FUN will each receive 10 percent of your current income.

For this step, you need to look at your current income and bills and ask, "How much of my income can I set aside each week in these two envelopes?" The percentages are the same, and I recommend you put an equal amount in each envelope. Remember, the amount does not matter right now; consistency is the key that makes this work! If all you can spare is a penny for each envelope, then put a penny in each envelope. The most important thing is to start putting money into these accounts today so you can see the amounts growing over time.

You may find that you are one of those people who need to 'see' their money grow to stick with this. That's okay!

For you, I suggest using plastic or glass jars instead of envelopes. You do not need anything fancy—just cut the top off a soda or juice bottle, use a thoroughly cleaned mayonnaise jar, or even set out a designated drinking glass. Just make sure to label each container like the envelopes and display them in a prominent place.

Note: This could be on a windowsill, a shelf in the kitchen, on the dresser in your bedroom, or even on the bathroom counter. The important thing is making sure they are in a place where you will see them at least once per day.

And remember, you aren't alone! Putting the two-liter bottles with the tops cut off on the counter in my bathroom where I saw them when I got ready for work in the morning and when I got ready for bed at night was very helpful for getting through some rough patches with my finances. For those who have bank accounts, the info in the jars could be bank statements or even slips of paper with dollar amounts on them.

Now that we have gotten started, let me explain what the categories on the envelopes mean.

Necessities (NEC-55%): As the name implies, this account is used to pay for day-to-day living expenses. It includes food, clothing, utilities, transportation (getting to and from work, going to the store, etc.), and a place to live.

Note: this percentage can be decreased to 50 percent, if you feel strongly about donating 10 percent of your income to charity.

Long-Term Savings for Spending (LTSS—10%): This account is meant to help you save for a long-term goal. For example, a new car, a down payment on a house, or even a child's college fund. It is for any item that cannot be paid for out of your current income.

Note: If you have more than one item you are saving for, such as a new car and the down payment on a house, create a second envelope and split the percentage. The envelope labeled "car" would receive 5 percent and the envelope labeled "down payment" would receive 5 percent, for a total of 10 percent in this category.

The percentages do not need to be split 50/50; they just cannot exceed 10 percent of current income.

> Tip—You may need more than 1 envelope to account for your long-term savings goals. Label each envelope with the appropriate goal and the percentage of current income going toward that goal.
>
> The total amount of money dedicated to this category is 10 percent of your total budget, maximum.

Retirement/Financial Freedom (RET—10%): This is the account that builds financial security, helping assure you will never be in money trouble again. As the name implies, it can be used for retirement in the traditional sense…but I like to think of it as my '*I work because I want to, not because I have to*' account.

The key to this account is to build your savings through regular investing. For example, if you regularly put $100 per month in this account for 5 years, the principal amount is going to be $6000. This is 60 months (5 years times 12 months in a year) times $100.

This is the place where you deposit any windfalls. Year-end bonus checks, spare change, money you found on the street—it should all go into the financial freedom account. You might be thinking why? The answer is simple. This is found money, you weren't expecting it so put it into an account where it can grow and move your financial goals forward.

Note: Retirement accounts have limits on how much you can contribute each year. Over time, you will max out your retirement contributions. At that point, your windfalls will go into a regular savings or an investment account.

This envelope is also where you should record all 401k, IRA, TSP, 403B or RRSP contributions. Simply put, these are the various names for retirement accounts companies set-up for their employees. Depositing 1-3 percent of your current gross income into your company's 401k plan will increase your savings without reducing your take home pay. The reason behind this anomaly is that the contribution (the money for the 401k and other company created retirement plans) is taken out of your paycheck before taxes are calculated. This is called a pre-tax deduction. As you get salary increases, also consider increasing your retirement contribution.

To calculate your take home pay, the company first subtracts your 401k contribution from your gross salary, then calculates the tax due on that amount. Because there is now less money being taxed, the net effect equals no change to your take home pay. In some cases, you may even see a small increase in your take home pay after contributing to the retirement plan! That disparity stops around 3 percent of your income and you will begin to see a decrease in your take home pay.

Note: Because of the tax savings, the decrease will be less than the amount put into the retirement plan. My recommendation is to increase your contribution each time you get a salary increase. This way you get an increase in your paycheck and your retirement plan.

This also means in April, when you are preparing your tax return, your tax bill will be lower because your income has been reduced by the amount of money you contributed to your 401k or other workplace retirement plan. This does not affect the salary amount used for social security or Medicare calculations.

When you are ready to withdraw money from your financial freedom account, only use the income, interest, dividends, etc. that have accumulated in the account and leave the principal intact. This ensures that your financial freedom account will continue to provide you with income for years to come.

The principal is any money that you have contributed to this account, whether it is in the form of 401k, IRA, or RRSP contributions or windfall deposits. Any money the account earned over the amount you deposited into the account is available to be spent.

As you age, you can have a discussion with your financial planner regarding leaving a legacy, dipping into principal and how to dispose of any assets that remain after you die.

Charity/Giving (GIVE—5%): I fully believe that we must help others any way we are able. This account is yours to give to people who may need help more than you do. You can donate money through your local church or a favorite cause, such as the American Heart Association or the American Diabetes Association, two of the charities I donate to.

There are some of you out there that say, "But I tithe!" For those unfamiliar with the term, tithing is when you give 10 percent of your income to charity. If this describes you, then you need to take the additional 5 percent from the necessity category. In your case, you will be working toward paying necessities with a total of 50 percent of your income instead of the 55 percent you will see mentioned throughout this book.

Education (ED—10%): This account is used to keep your skills current. It is not limited to your current job skills. These savings can pay for financial training you might be interested in, such as real estate investing or stock market investing to name a few.

Maybe you would like to start a business. Take some classes before plunging in. Find out what is involved from a local technical college or community college. If you are really unsure what courses to take, check out free seminars and webinars.

Free courses are a great way to meet new people and learn a new skill. Many times you get to try the skill in class and can get an idea of whether you would enjoy using that skill either in a job or your own business.

Fun (FUN–10%): This account is your reward for following your plan. It is for you to use once a month to do something FUN! In the beginning, some of you may only have twenty-five cents in this account and ask, "What can I get with that?"

Consider things like Bazooka bubble gum. You can chew the sugary sweet gum and blow bubbles while reading the comics inside. You can learn how to play card games. You could even practice sleight of hand tricks!

As time passes, things will improve. There will be more money in the FUN envelope, and soon you will be having your hair colored at a fancy beauty salon or spending a day at a spa. This is your release valve.

You have been scrimping and saving to improve your financial future, you do not want to get frustrated and blow all your hard work. You want to let the little kid inside you have fun every so often or frustration will sabotage your efforts.

So please, follow this suggestion and find some way to have low-cost or no cost FUN *each month* in the beginning! Do not save up because your inner voice/wild child/younger you will rebel, and you *will* decide that retail therapy splurge, a wild night on the town or some other large expenditure will make you feel better. Then, suddenly, you'll find your financial picture is even worse than it was before. So please find a way to have fun and keep your inner child happy!

SUMMARY

In this chapter, you have learned:

- To identify long-term uses for money and create a way to keep track of that
- Having FUN is as important as knowing where your money is going.

In the next chapter, you will learn about budgets.

CHAPTER FOUR

FOUR MONTHS LATER

"The man who moves a mountain begins
by carrying away small stones."

—**Confucius**

Materials Required:

- Copy of the sample budget in Appendix A
- Blank budget form, either from Appendix B or a budget form you have used in the past
- List of all your income and where it comes from
- List of all your bills, due dates, and the total amount due
- Calculator
- 1 hour of uninterrupted time

Okay, you have now used the money in your FUN account twice. Did you enjoy it? Did you let go and feel the kid inside you? Are you beginning to see the power of saving a little at a time and watching how it adds up?

Good! Because today, we are going to discuss budgeting and cash management techniques.

I know many of you heard me say 'budgets' and your eyes automatically started glazing over. Personally, I like numbers. I also know we all have things we are good at and things we hate. However, working with budgets does not need to be challenging. You are going to use the information you have been gathering over the last 4 months to build this plan.

Pull out the remaining four envelopes or your recent bank statement showing your accounts.

You will see a sample budget in Appendix A and a blank budget form in Appendix B. You can copy the blank budget and fill in your information. If you already have a form you prefer, you can use that instead.

As you can see, I have split the budget items under the appropriate envelope headings. This allows you to know precisely why you are putting money in that envelope and prevents conflicting ideas from sabotaging your efforts.

For those who are visual, you will use the remaining 4 clear plastic containers that you labeled in Chapter Three.

Today's assignment is to look at the sample budget and create one of your own. It does not have to be fancy, but it does need to be written. Written goals can be displayed and pursued. If it's just in your head, consider it dead. By having your budget goals written and displayed in a prominent place, you will find it harder for anything to sidetrack you. You can point to your budget and your progress on your goals to help dissuade you from spending money on things not on your list, especially those items that aren't going to help you reach your goal of financial independence.

I understand that after two months many of you are still finding that 99 percent of income goes toward paying for necessities. Don't be discouraged if the percentages on your first budget are skewed and the amount going toward your long-term goals looks terribly inadequate. Do not despair. Rome was not built in a day.

Becoming financially free and able to do what you want, when you want, will not happen overnight. The fact is, if you keep doing what you have been doing, you will keep getting what you have been getting. You picked up this book because you wanted something different for your life. Creating a budget, and using it, is the next step in that process.

There are some of you that picked up this book or were given a copy by a friend and thought, "another dry dusty financial book to clutter up my home," or "I am hopeless with finances/money just ask my husband." I hope that you are starting to see that with proper instruction, you too can make sense of this financial stuff.

Now that you have completed your budget by putting dollar amounts next to each item on your budget form along with the headings for each of the six envelopes, it is time to split your paycheck into each of your envelopes or see through containers. You will see on the sample budget that the percentages are also listed for each of the envelopes. For those of you struggling to make ends meet, split up the percentages for the dollar amount you can afford for the five categories after necessities.

For example:

Assume you make $1000 per week take home and $990.00 is used for necessities. This leaves $10.00 to split between the other envelopes. As necessities are 55 percent of our ideal budget, then that $10.00 represents 45 percent of our ideal budget. This means that:

		Today	Future
Necessities	(55%)	$990.00	$550.00
Fun	(10%)	2.22	100.00
Charity	(05%)	1.12	50.00
Retirement	(10%)	2.22	100.00
Long-term savings	(10%)	2.22	100.00
Education	(10%)	2.22	100.00
Total:		$1000.00	$1000.00

For those wondering how I came up with the percentages, the math is as follows:

FUN = 10% of the ideal budget or 10% out of 100% or 1/10

However, we do not have 100 percent to work with we only have 45 percent left to work with for the remaining 5 envelopes so the math changes from 10 percent divided by 100 percent to 10 percent divided by 45 percent

This yields:

(10/45) * $10.00 = 2.22222

Or as a word problem

(10 divided by 45) times $10.00 equals 2.2222

As money only consists of 2 decimal places, the number becomes 2.22 or $2.22.

I agree the numbers look so small that you are probably saying to yourself, "why bother? I will start later when I make more money, when I can put more in each account. What can you buy with two dollars and twenty-two cents ($2.22)? What is the point?"

The answer is simple.

Start today at whatever level you can. You are working on a plan for life, not something you do once and forget about.

Look at the following chart to illustrate the power of starting early. If you start with a penny and the penny is doubled every time period (day/week/month/ year) at the end of 30 time periods, you will have over 5 million dollars.

CHART 1

Time Period	Amount Invested	Interest Earned	Total
1	$0.01		
2		$00.01	00.02
3		00.02	00.04
4		00.04	00.08
5		00.08	00.16
6		00.16	00.32
7		00.32	00.64
8		00.64	01.28
9		01.28	02.56
10		02.56	05.12
11		05.12	10.24
12		10.24	20.48
13		20.48	40.96
14		40.96	81.92
15		81.92	163.84
16		163.84	327.68
17		327.68	655.36
18		655.36	1,310.72
19		1,310.72	2,621.44
20		2,621.44	5,242.88
21		5,242.88	10,485.76
22		10,485.76	20,971.52
23		20,971.52	41,943.04
24		41,943.04	83,866.08
25		83,866.08	167,772.16
26		167,772.16	335,544.32
27		335,544.32	671,088.64
28		671,088.64	1,342,172.20
29		1,342,172.20	2,684,354.40
30		2,684,354.40	5,368,708.80

Note: This chart discusses doubling your money. This is not depositing twice as much in an envelope today over what you put in yesterday.

What this chart shows is called compounding. It is how money grows in an interest bearing account when no withdrawals are made.

As you can see in the beginning, the amounts look tiny. "Why bother?" quickly springs to mind. However, when you get to time period (day/week/ month/year) 21, you have over $10,000 in your account doing nothing more than investing one (1) penny and doubling it over time.

The chart can be used in any calendar denomination, i.e. days, weeks, months, or years, to show the power of getting started today. As most of you know, it is "easy" to save $1000; you have done that plenty of times already. It is keeping it that has been the hard part.

Something always comes up, the kids need shoes, braces, the car needs an oil change, new tires, you are throwing a birthday party and need extra groceries and a birthday present, the church needs a new roof and is asking for donations. You say to yourself this is just a temporary setback, I will replace it soon.

If you look at Chart 1, you see that $81.92 corresponds to time period 14 and if left to compound seven more times would have become over $10,000. Compounding is the growth of money kept in an interest bearing account that earns interest on both the accumulated interest and the principal amount invested.

At some point, you will have between $100 and $500 in an envelope. At that time you will want to open an interest-bearing bank account. We did not discuss opening a bank account earlier due to the fees the bank charges if you don't maintain a minimum balance in your account. Shop around to find a bank that will let you open an account with a minimum balance and the lowest fees.

For those comfortable with online only banking there are a number of online banks with low initial opening balances and low or no monthly fees.

Do your due diligence and make sure the online bank offers the services you need and is a legitimate business and not a scam.

I know it is not easy to "hide" money from yourself. I too let today's worries intrude on my tomorrow's freedom. I too lived paycheck-to-paycheck wondering where the money was going, wondering how there could be so much month left at the end of each paycheck.

Then I got divorced. That fear of being homeless and living off social security at age 65 was a vision I refused to accept for my future. So, I decided to do whatever it took to create a different future for myself. First, I created a budget and forced myself to live within it. This meant no more Starbucks Mocha Grandes. No more eating at fancy restaurants. It meant shopping at the grocery store with a list, eating at home and brown bagging lunch at work. But I am well on my way to a secure future and you can be too.

As the Nike commercial says, "Just Do It." The trick is to start. The amount is not important. Getting started on a disciplined savings program is what is important. If you have to start your financial freedom/retirement account with a piggybank that you hide in your sock drawer, do it.

Teach your kids the importance of savings. If they start early, they could buy their own car, save enough to pay for college and have a financial freedom account that will allow them more choices in choosing a career and what to do with their lives.

Budgeting is not easy. I do not mean the act of creating one. You can use the blank form in the back of this book or buy printed ones at the department store or even Etsy with all the items you could imagine already listed in neat columns for you. The hard part is to continue following the budget once it is created.

The long-term goals are the ones that tend to suffer when a short-term emergency arises. The down payment for a house or money to replace/buy a car is raided to pay for the root canal or new tires for the current car.

What you should try instead is arrange a payment plan or use a credit card to cover these expenses. If either of these options is unavailable, consider going to your bank and applying for a loan. Many banks will offer up to $5,000 unsecured to customers, with the amount dependent on credit history and your track record with the bank.

For more detailed information how to pay for emergencies see Appendix C.

The key is to create a realistic budget and stick with it. This is your greatest weapon against retiring on social security and living at, or below, the poverty level. You are building up savings and investments so you can supplement your social security payments. The other option is to work until you are too old and infirm to work any longer and end up relying on the government to take care of your needs.

To me relying on the government is a very unappealing option and I'm sure it is to you as well. So much for that traveling to exotic lands, visiting the grandkids, and all the other things you dreamed about doing after you retired. Decide now, which reality you want for your future. Do you want poverty and/or working until you die or financial independence?

My suggestion is to post the budget somewhere you can see it every day, bathroom mirror, wall in your home office, wall behind the desk where you pay the bills, anywhere you can see how things are going at a glance. I also suggest color-coding the budget so you can easily tell what has been paid even from across the room.

Always deposit something into long-term savings and the retirement/financial freedom accounts. It is critical to your continuing on the path to financial freedom to see progress in these two areas. It is especially important to utilize the Fun envelope once a month. This keeps the kid inside you happy and makes the tough choices easier to accept. Don't forget to reward yourself for sticking with your budget.

SUMMARY

In this chapter, you learned:

- about budgets
- created a budget using your information.
- to print and hang your budget in a prominent place as a reminder of where you are and where you are going.

In the next chapter, we will discuss long-term career plans.

CHAPTER FIVE

SIX MONTHS LATER

"You educate a man; you educate a man. You educate a woman; you educate a generation."

—**Brigham Young**

Materials Required:

- Blank paper
- Pen or pencil
- 30 uninterrupted minutes

Another two months have gone by. You now have six months' worth of savings in your retirement/financial freedom account. Six months ago, all your money was going to necessities and you could not see the light at the end of the tunnel. Now you see money accumulating toward long-term goals and it feels wonderful.

You have also been living with a budget for the last two months. It is freeing you from worry, while showing you a path to better times.

There is money accumulating in all six envelopes. Two envelopes, Necessities and FUN are being spent every month. You are feeling more confident about your ability to handle money. You have a more positive outlook on life in general.

You realize that you are able to create a budget. You can save money for a long-term goal. You are no longer worrying all the time about living paycheck to paycheck forever. Your positive mental attitude makes you friendlier at work. You are getting more done, and this is getting you noticed.

The exercise for this section is to get clear on your career goals. Where do you see yourself in 6 months, one year, even five years from now? Do you see yourself as the manager of your current department in five years? Or lead sales rep training the new sales reps? Or do you see yourself running your own business in five years after learning what you can from your current employer?

Also list any job skills that could be transferable to another department or company. For example, programming skills, knowledge of software such as Microsoft office suite, even software unique to the industry you are in are transferable skills. Do not edit yourself, just write everything down, everything that you know and do in your current job and you can sort through the list later when creating an updated resume.

The purpose of this exercise is to get a crystal clear vision of your future. This vision will be used to create your roadmap which in turn will lead to your becoming whatever it is you wrote down in your brainstorming session.

Stop and do the exercise now

Now that you are clear on where you want to be five years from now, review your current job situation. If you do not see a career path leading from your current position, it is time to start researching opportunities for someone with your skills. Sometimes, the opportunity will be in a different department or division of the company you work for. Other times, your career will require leaving your current company. Yes, this is a big step. However, you have spent the last four months working on your finances and are ready to expand your horizons.

If you like and trust your current boss, and the work you are doing, you might consider having a talk with your boss about your career plans. Ask for his/her help to make them a reality.

He/She might schedule training classes or let you work on a joint project with another department. He/she might point out that this is what we do here and the opportunity you are asking about is not possible here. You should not be upset or even hint at leaving at this point. These actions could jeopardize your future with this company and you need to keep this job while you search for the next one.

Thank your boss for taking the time to speak with you and ask him/her to keep you in mind if something that you discussed becomes available. Make sure your boss knows that you want to learn new things, while helping them do a better job.

Remember, if you are working for a company that builds widgets but you really want to be a waitress, discussing your career plans with your boss will not get you what you want. Do some research about your own company. Your research will show if your career plans can happen at your current company. If the research shows your plans are possible, consider discussing your long-term career plans with your boss.

After deciding that there is no advancement possibility at the company you are at now, it is time to begin a job search. There are many good books on that subject so I recommend you go to the library and take advantage of the resources available there.

Or do an online search for more information on opportunities that you listed in your brainstorming session. Keep in mind that information found on the internet is not always accurate. Do not rely on just one website to give you the information you are seeking.

Furthermore, unless you are changing fields with no relevant experience or education in that field, you likely will command an increased salary in your new position.

Remember, statistically women make approximately 83 cents on the dollar to a man's salary. The reason for this fact is two-fold. Many times women will interrupt their career to take care of young children or elderly parents. In other cases, a woman "acts" like she doesn't need the money or just accepts whatever salary is offered without considering what she is really worth.

If you don't feel comfortable with salary negotiations, don't forget there are many books on that subject. Pick one up while at the library and be the best prepared candidate at your next job interview. Or go to Amazon and buy a book you can own and mark up as necessary. The choice is yours.

In the beginning I mentioned using the library more than going online as libraries have a lot of free resources available to everyone. And there are generally knowledgeable staff at the library that can also help you in your search for information. And if you don't have your own smartphone or computer, libraries also offer computers with internet access to help you with your online searches.

SUMMARY

In this chapter you:

- Brainstormed job and career choices.
- Gained clarity about who you are and what you want from an employer.
- Started preparing a plan for how to achieve your long-term career goals and the next step to take in that plan.

CHAPTER SIX

EIGHT MONTHS LATER

"I did then what I knew how to do.
Now that I know better, I do better."

- **Maya Angelou**

Materials Required:

- Current budget
- 30 uninterrupted minutes

You found a new job or negotiated a new opportunity at your current company. Congratulations. It is now time to adjust the budget to account for the new income. Do not increase the amount of your income going into the necessities envelope.

All new income is to be split between the other five envelopes. The long-term goal is that only 55 percent of income pays for necessities. Over time with salary increases, bonuses and other additional income sources, this goal will be achieved. Split any additional income that you receive between the remaining five envelopes and maintain the current necessities budget.

It is very important to avoid a "keeping up with the Jones" mentality and live within your budget constraints. Keeping your eye on the prize, in this case, only working because you want to, not because you have to, should help you stay on track.

You also do not want to jeopardize your long-term goals such as owning your own home or sending your children to college by splurging on items that do not help you reach these long-term goals.

By not keeping up with the Jones I am suggesting that now is not the time to splurge on a new wardrobe or rush out and buy a new car. If however, this is a long-term goal you have been saving for and you have saved enough in the LTSS envelope to pay for one of these goals then by all means get the new wardrobe, car, etc.

It is very tempting to increase spending when the paycheck increases and you should be disciplined enough by now to see how that will hurt you in the long run.

So stay the course. Follow your current budget with the increased income going toward increased savings. Note how much sooner you will reach your long-term goals.

Also, notice your stress level has decreased. Your bills are being paid, more money is being set aside for long-term goals and emergencies don't cause the panic they used to.

The really astounding thing is that the new job and added responsibilities are not only making you feel more confident in your abilities but making you realize that fearing money and all things financial was your parents issue and is no longer yours.

SUMMARY

In this chapter, you

- Reviewed your existing budget and made changes to it based on your new salary.
- Realized you are becoming a confident and financially savvy woman.

CHAPTER SEVEN

ONE YEAR LATER

"It had long since come to my attention
that people of accomplishment rarely sat
back and let things happen to them. They
went out and happened to things."

- **Leonardo da Vinci**

Materials Required:

- Smartphone/Computer with Internet Connection
- Highlighter
- Blank paper
- 1 uninterrupted hour

One year has gone by. It's hard to believe you have lived within a budget, have money set aside for long-term goal(s) and retirement. You have spent the money in the FUN envelope every month and have had some really interesting experiences.

You see that good things come to those who are prepared. A while back, you got a great promotion at work, or you left that dead-end job for a great new career. All lights are green; everything is looking up.

You check the budget, your long-term savings account, labeled down payment, and decide now is the time to buy a house. As further incentive your landlord just stopped by with a notice stating in 30 days your rent will be increasing 10 percent. You decide to do some internet searches and see what's available to buy or rent.

While skimming through the items that came up in your search, you come across an ad that says 'Rent to own. Open house this weekend'. The rent they are asking for is what you are paying now and you wonder what 'rent to own' means. Your curiosity is piqued so you decide to attend the open house.

The house is near where you live now. It has a large backyard, 3 bedrooms, and 1-1/2 bathrooms. It is an older home that needs some cosmetic work, but appears to be structurally sound. There is a brochure on the kitchen counter, and a few other couples are there asking questions of the real estate agent. You read the brochure and it says:

> Rent $800.00 per month with 1-year lease,
>
> security deposit $1600
>
> Or
>
> Lease option $4,000 (goes toward down payment)
>
> Sales price $150,000
>
> Must complete deal within 1 year or option is forfeit.
>
> Rent $800 per month. Will apply $200 per month credit toward the down payment.

You are not sure what this means, but the real estate agent is busy talking with other couples. His name is on the brochure, so you decide to leave and make an appointment with your banker.

You bring the brochure to the appointment and ask the banker to explain it to you. He is familiar with your situation since he helped you with a short-term loan earlier this year which you paid on time every month. The banker considers you a good customer and more importantly a good credit risk.

Your banker explains that option 1 is a typical rental situation. You would sign a lease for 1 year and pay $800 per month to live there. You also put up a $1600 security deposit, which is refunded to you at the end of the lease, if the property is in the same condition as when you moved in. Meaning you clean the place, do not damage the walls, floors or other fixtures or leave trash behind that the landlord has to remove before they can rent the property.

Option 2 is called a lease option or rent to own. In this case, you pay $4000 to secure the option to buy the house for $150,000 within 1 year. The $4000 is a cash payment called an option, not a security deposit and is nonrefundable if you decide you do not want to buy the house within 1 year.

The rent is the same in both cases, but the owner has agreed to credit $200 of the rent toward the down payment. This means that at the end of the year you would have $4000, from the option plus $2400 from the rent credit or a total of $6400 toward the down payment on this house.

Now that you understand their offer, you ask the banker about your ability to qualify for a loan. He asks for your current salary and any other income sources. He confirms you paid back the short-term loan on time and verifies you have no other outstanding debt.

He then says he can pre-qualify you for a $135,000 mortgage. That means the bank will loan you up to $135,000 to buy a house. The bank will loan up to 90 percent of the purchase price. This means that you qualify to buy a $150,000 house with a $15,000 down payment.

As he knows you are new to buying real estate, he also recommends that you go to the library and local real estate offices to review literature on real estate transactions. He gives you some suggestions of websites that could be helpful to visit. He then proceeds to give you a high-level overview of how a typical real estate transaction works.

1. Find a house you like
2. Put a contract on the house, contingent on home inspection, mortgage qualification, other items that you feel are needed to protect your rights and a small deposit to bind your offer
3. If your offer is accepted, line up the professionals needed to fulfill the contingency requirements including calling your banker to get a mortgage.

   Note: Some of these items can be done in advance, such as getting a pre-qualification letter from the bank.
4. The real estate agent and banker work with a title company to close the loan
5. You go to the title company/banker's office, sign the mortgage papers and get the keys to your new home

With the lease option there is one final twist. You can live in the house for 1 year and decide at the end to either buy it or walk away. If you walk away or find you cannot secure the remaining down payment or financing in time, you lose the option money, in this case $4000.

So the decision is yours. Stay where you are and pay the increased rent for the coming year. Agree to rent the house for the same rent you are paying now or take the lease option and agree to buy the house at some point in the coming year.

Do not rush into this. If you are close to saving the remaining $8,600 toward the down payment and you like the neighborhood, then my recommendation is buy the house.

Review your existing budget and see how much has been saved in the LTSS account labeled house down payment. Also, check with your

HR representative about the ability to borrow against the money in your 401k account to buy a first home. This is one of the exceptions available to first time home buyers.

If you decide to borrow money from the 401k you will then be required to pay yourself back over time. As long as you remain at your current company you can make payments to the plan. However, if you decide to leave the company, you are required to pay the loan in full when you leave. If you cannot pay it in full before you leave then the amount still due on the loan is treated as a withdrawal and if you are under 59-1/2 you will pay taxes on the amount not paid back and a 10 percent early withdrawal penalty.

If you find that you cannot come up with the difference you need to fund the down payment, consider looking at a home with a lower sales price. Or if you really want this home and realize that you could come up with the needed down payment in a slightly longer time period, say 18 months, consider putting in a contract stating that you would like to buy the house in 18 months with all the other terms remaining the same.

If however, it would take a miracle to come up with that much cash in less than 1 year do not consider the lease option. You will end up losing $4,000 and will beat yourself up for years over your financial failings. If you don't take this deal, there will be another one later. Budgeting and saving are a long-term strategy, not a get rich quick scheme.

SUMMARY

In this chapter, you learned

- about reading real estate ads
- you researched buying real estate and qualifying for a mortgage.

CHAPTER EIGHT

TWO YEARS LATER

"The speed of your success is limited
only by your dedication and what
you're willing to sacrifice"

- **Nathan W. Morris**

Materials Required:

- Blank paper
- Pencil/Pen
- 1 uninterrupted hour

It is now decision time. Some of you took the path of least resistance and chose to stay in the apartment despite the rent increase. You recently received a 30-day notice stating the rent was again increasing 10 percent over last year.

Some of you moved to the house and signed a one-year lease. You just received a 30-day notice to vacate the premises. The owner of the property found a buyer and the new owners would like to live in the property.

Still others of you decided to buy the house under the lease option agreement. You checked your budget, your long-term savings and had the bank's prequalification letter to back up your decision.

You always liked the neighborhood. The house had a big yard for family get-togethers and relaxation and is near work. You signed the 1-year lease option. You paid $4000 for the option and $1200 per month rent, $200 of which was applied toward the down payment. You spent the last 11 months adding to savings to reach your down payment goal of $8,600. You are working with your banker to ensure the financing is in place. Over the year, you have had a number of family get-togethers and realized how much you want to own this house. You call the real estate agent and ask to set a closing date. You are ready to complete the sale.

As part of the bank's process to get your mortgage approved, they have an appraisal done. Based on comparable sales in the neighborhood over the last year, your new home is worth $160,000. Just by agreeing to buy the house for $150,000 last year, you already have $10,000 in equity. Though this is common in a good market, do not agree to a lease option expecting this to happen. If it does, that is great.

Real estate historically has increased in value 5 percent per year when held long-term. If you buy property right, using logic rather than emotions, not only do you get a place to call home but you also have a built in savings plan that is easy to forget about.

Later, we will see how the money in your home can be turned into savings and investment capital.

For now, you buy the house and if possible get a fixed-rate mortgage. This way, regardless of how interest rates, the economy, even your salary change, you always know what your mortgage payment will be.

If you know that you will be looking for a new house in a few years, due to having more children or needing more space for elderly parents, then my personal recommendation is to consider a 5-year or 7-year ARM (adjustable rate mortgage) with as low a cap as possible. A cap refers to how many percentage points can be added to or subtracted from your current interest rate each year. It also refers to how high the maximum interest rate can rise.

For example, assume a 5-year ARM at 4-1/2 percent with an annual cap of 2 percent, maximum lifetime interest rate of 10-1/2 percent, minimum interest rate of 3 percent. This means for the first 5 years of the mortgage the interest rate will be 4-1/2 percent and the payment will be a fixed amount for those 5 years.

At the end of 5 years or 60 months, the rate will adjust. In our example, the rate can go either up 2 percent or down 2 percent–that is what the annual cap means. However, the interest rate can never go lower than 3 percent or higher than 101/2 percent–the minimum and maximum interest rates specified in the contract.

After the first 5 years, this type of mortgage can adjust once per year on your anniversary date. This is why if you plan to stay in a property long-term I recommend a fixed rate loan.

As you can see from this example, if you plan to move within 5 years, then a 5 year ARM yields predictable payments. More importantly the 5 year ARM acts like a fixed rate loan usually at a lower interest rate and thus lower monthly cost for the first five years. Five years gives you time to decide whether to keep the property or sell it prior to the rate changing.

Short-term ARMS (anything under 5 years) can be used if there is no other way to qualify for a mortgage but they are notorious for jumping the maximum number of points, i.e. whatever the cap is, 2 percent in our example, at the first rate change.

If selecting a 1 year ARM in order to qualify for the mortgage, ask the banker to calculate what your payment would be if the rate changed to the maximum, in this case 4-1/2 percent plus 2 percent equals 6-1/2 percent.

If you do not believe your salary would increase enough to be able to afford that kind of increase then I suggest not buying the house at that point. The last thing you want to do is lose the house when you can no longer make the monthly payments.

A foreclosure would mar your otherwise good credit history and will stay on your record for the next seven to ten years, possibly longer, making buying a home in the future more difficult.

For further discussion on home ownership options, continue to the next chapter.

SUMMARY

In this chapter, you learned:

- Pros and cons of renting vs. buying a home.
- The differences between adjustable rate mortgages and fixed-rate mortgages and under what circumstances you would use each type of loan.

CHAPTER NINE

FOUR YEARS LATER

"Nothing has meaning except for
the meaning you give it."

- **T. Harv Eker,** *Secrets of the Millionaire Mind: Mastering the Inner Game of Wealth*

Materials Required:

- Current budget
- Current account balances
- Blank paper Pen/pencil
- 30 uninterrupted minutes

Hard to believe, two more years have gone by. Congratulations to those of you who bought a home. You have built up equity by paying your mortgage on time every month. An added plus is the area you are living in has become very desirable further increasing your property value.

If you are still renting, you should have a decent balance in both the long-term saving and financial freedom/retirement accounts. By now, even in the worst circumstances you could be close to buying a home.

Some people will tell you that a bankruptcy on your record will make it impossible for you to buy a house. Some say trouble with the law makes you unemployable or a credit risk. Whatever else the naysayers are saying; just STOP listening.

Remember, when you first picked up this book four years ago, you did not have two nickels to rub together. Today, you have a personal banker, a savings account earmarked for buying a home; a long-term investment plan and you are working with your banker to get qualified for a mortgage.

Maybe your first home will be a mobile home, a condominium (condo) or a townhouse rather than a single family home. That is okay. You have to start somewhere. There are pros and cons to all forms of ownership. With a condominium, all exterior maintenance, landscaping, garbage pickup, etc is handled by someone else. Plus many complexes have a fitness center, swimming pool, and game room for the owners to use. A monthly condominium fee covers everything from exterior maintenance to amenities. Your only responsibility, besides paying the monthly fee, is to maintain the inside of your unit.

Condominiums also tend to be secure buildings with keyed entryways and security guards. These are great for people who travel a lot, do not like yard work and especially the elderly.

Townhouses are two or more attached single-family homes. Townhouses typically share common ground and have a contract with someone to handle landscaping/yard work and garbage pickup. Often there are covenants (agreements) regarding the color you can paint your townhouse (exterior), where you can park, how the common property is maintained and used.

Unlike a condominium, the owners in a town-home community are responsible for the upkeep of their unit both inside and outside. There often is a master contract that all the owners agree to covering major exterior items. This includes roof repair, shingle or siding upkeep, as these items are shared among the owners and proper maintenance keeps everyone's property values high.

Mobile homes and single-family homes are similar in that everything is your responsibility. Mowing the lawn, painting the house, arranging trash pickup, etc. are all your jobs. If you are interested in security, you hire the security company or put up a fence.

You want a pool. You either buy a home that has one or you contract with an installer to have one built. Once it is built, you are responsible for maintaining the chemicals, keeping it clean and usable. Want a fitness room, you build it and buy equipment, or join a fitness club. The advantage is you have more privacy than other forms of ownership, and it is all yours. You want to park cars on the lawn, it is your choice.

Before buying a single-family home in a subdivision, you do need to confirm if there is a homeowners' association. Homeowner association rules and regulations can vary. Some associations are similar to a townhouse association that spell out everything you can and cannot do on your property. Others are a short document specifying exterior house paint color schemes and asking people to maintain their property.

Read thoroughly the association documents prior to buying to ensure your happiness after you move into your new home.

There are some of you saying "but I do not want the hassles of ownership. I pay my rent on time and if there is a problem, I call the landlord. He unstops the toilet, changes the light bulbs, and paints the bedroom. I can leave this property at the end of lease and go elsewhere. I do not want to be tied down..."

I understand these arguments, some of them I even used myself, but let us get back to the original premise of this book, you want to be financially free to do what you want, when you want. You do not want to be tied to a nine to five (9-5) job. Owning real estate is just another piece of the puzzle on your road to financial independence.

I will show a little later how you can get tax-free income from your home while you continue to live there. You cannot do that while you rent and pay someone else's mortgage for them.

SUMMARY

In this chapter you learned:

- The various home ownership options from condominiums to single-family homes
- Pros and cons of each type of ownership.

CHAPTER TEN

SIX YEARS LATER

"Children must be taught how to
think, not what to think."

- **Margaret Mead**

Materials Required:

- Gather children 5 years old and up
- Box of #10 business envelopes
- 1 Black marker per child
- 1 uninterrupted hour

For those of you with children at least 5 years old, now is the time to get them involved with a savings program. Explain to them the meaning of the various envelopes and percentages and why it is important to start now. Make it a game.

Explain the necessities envelope and point out that while they live under your roof, the money for necessities, such as food and clothing, a roof over their head, is your responsibility. And that until they are old enough to get a job, write a book, find a way to earn income, then you will pay for all necessities.

However, once they have income, you should discuss with the child contributing money for their room and board, clothing, and other items that are considered necessities. This helps prepare them for the 'real' world, and more importantly, helps with their self-image and self-esteem.

The younger children will find the retirement/financial freedom account the most confusing. To them retirement is something old people do, like grandma and grandpa and not working for a living is hard to comprehend because all the adults they come in contact with talk about work and jobs.

To get this concept across, I recommend using examples of very public, very successful people. For example, Elon Musk and Donald Trump are in the news, larger-than-life people that not only have lots of money but also do what they want when they want to.

They do not have to work. They choose to run corporations, not because they need the money to meet day-to-day living expenses but instead so they can give to the community while working on projects that interest them. This leads to their donating large sums of money to charitable foundations or lending their name and/or support to various causes.

This also ties into the charity/giving envelope. In the beginning, the children really will not understand the concept of donating money to charity. It is too abstract a concept.

However, you can bring them to a veteran's hospital or an old age/ retirement home and show them how visiting these people brightens their day. Maybe your child likes animals; if they are old enough, they might be able to volunteer at the local animal shelter. Be creative in showing them how the things they are interested in might help others.

The long-term savings account can be used for a new bike or for older children, a first car. It teaches children restraint as they can see if they spend the money on movies, CD-ROMs or video games today, they cannot afford the bike or car later. This also requires you to hold your ground.

If you agree to pay $100 toward the bike if the child saves $100 you cannot decide to buy it for them anyway because you just got a bonus at work. We are creating self-sufficient, self-aware financially responsible adults. Do not feel that you are lacking because you are not buying the bike, automobile, etc. for the child.

My personal experience is that things that I worked to pay for myself are much more valuable to me than things that people gave me. This will also be true for your children.

The education envelope will be for special classes, summer camp programs, and after-school activities. The normal education expenses are still your responsibility as the parent.

However, ballet lessons, basketball camp, or any other extracurricular activity your child is interested in should be something the child contributes to. They will come away with greater insights into the material if they pick the activity and pay for it. They will value it much more than if you force them to go somewhere and participate in some activity that you alone pay for.

This does not mean the child must come up with the total cost of the new program. Just that they contribute to the cost. Each activity can be reviewed and who pays how much of the cost is decided when the child asks to participate.

The FUN envelope will need no explanation. The only problem will be if you feel the need to supplement the money in the envelope when the child goes to the store and finds they do not have enough money in the envelope for something they want.

It is tempting to solve the short-term whining with cash but this lets the child believe that complaining and whining is how to get ahead in this world. This is not what we are striving for. This envelope is meant to be used monthly. It is meant for having fun and is what makes putting money in the other envelopes bearable.

For a child, Christmas and their birthday takes forever to come, even though they happen on the same days each year, and they do not last long enough when they do come.

Again, the money in the FUN envelope is to be used any way the child wants. It should not be used for an educational movie you want your child to see. You should not belittle the child for what they choose to spend the money on or force them to choose something you think is more appropriate.

In the beginning, it will be tempting to try to control how your child uses the money in the envelopes. I agree that parents have the right to keep the child from buying pornographic material or violent video games; however, dictating what the child can do with the money is not helpful. Set boundaries based on the child's age and characteristics but trust them to spend the money in the FUN envelope as they see fit. This will also lead to greater harmony at home.

Your children will see you respect their wishes and will be less rebellious and more amenable to helping out around the house.

Remember, kids are inquisitive and soak up new ideas like a sponge. When presented in a clear and reasonable manner, children will treat the envelopes like a valuable tool.

They will come to understand that money doesn't grow on trees and you won't need to use that saying when you are shopping with your children. You can also make more informed decisions on family vacation choices if you explain what you are saving toward and get the children's input. I am not suggesting that the children should have veto power over the family budget, just that major decisions, such as Disney World for 2 weeks or a swimming pool in the backyard, might be topics to discuss as a family. You may be surprised what your kids think and this will lead to less stress and resentment.

SUMMARY

This chapter teaches:

- Children 5 years and older, the value of saving money.
- Children how to use this system.

CHAPTER ELEVEN

TEN YEARS LATER

"There is only one success—to be able
to spend life in your own way."

- **Christopher Morley**

Materials Required:

- List of High school choices in your area
- College catalogs
- SmartPhone/Computer and internet connection
- 1 uninterrupted hour

For some of you, the house you bought more than 5 years ago has become too small for your growing family.

For others, it's time to start researching high schools or colleges for your older children.

For still others, job promotions have led to you having to decide whether to move out of state or even out of the country or stay where you are with the possibility of being sidelined from the fast track.

When you started on this track ten years ago, you had trouble making ends meet each month. Now there is money in retirement accounts and long-term savings accounts. More importantly, less than 55 percent of your income is used to pay for necessities.

So let us review the options by starting with those needing a new home.

As you may remember when you bought your first home there are three different ownership options, condo, townhome or single family home. To review the various types of home ownership you can return to Chapter Ten.

It is true, you have a substantially higher income than when you bought your first home. You should not run out and buy an expensive home in a new neighborhood that will cause your necessities category to exceed 55 percent of your income. Needing a new home to house a growing family or desiring a home in a better neighborhood does not mean you should ignore your budget and the percentages on the envelopes to make that happen.

> **Tip:** Remember, you are currently enjoying a comfortable lifestyle with little stress and few money worries. You promised yourself that you would never put yourself in the position that you were ten years ago, living paycheck to paycheck and hoping for the best.

So, do the research using the search function on a website like Zillow.com or Realtor.com to find your new home but keep in mind how the new mortgage payment will impact your budget.

For those with children looking at choices for high school I would recommend reviewing the literature from each of the schools. After narrowing down your choices I recommend spending the day attending classes before making your final decision.

What is in the literature, even conversations with parents whose children are currently attending the school, are not sufficient to base your decision on. Check it out yourself.

Due diligence and knowledge of your child is also my recommendation for colleges. I am not going to suggest that all children should start at a school close to home. That only after proving they are responsible during that first year, look into colleges farther away.

Some children are naturally gregarious and can fit in anywhere. They have a drive to succeed and know what they want from an educational experience.

Other children are timid and would prefer living at home and attending a school they can drive to everyday.

Go to the library and find out what schools offer the program your child says he/she is interested in. Or use the search function on your computer or smartphone to do the research. Contact the schools you are interested in or watch the virtual tour. You can make the search as narrow or broad as you feel appropriate.

Visit the colleges websites and see what they have to say. Many times the college website includes links to testimonials from former and current students.

Once you and your child have narrowed down the choices, contact the school again to arrange a tour. If the college is out of state or sufficiently far from your home that your child will need to live on campus, ask the college to arrange for an upperclassman to entertain your child for one night in the dorm, preferably a student in the same program your child is interested in.

Review the experience with your child the next day and listen to what they have to say. If your child tells you they liked the classes, the people, and think they could get used to living in the dorm, don't make them feel guilty about choosing to leave home. On the other hand if your child is upset about being left overnight then you should concentrate on finding colleges near home so your child can come home at night and does not need to stay in a dorm.

My best suggestion on colleges is to listen to your child. They know what they want and in most cases will be honest with you. As the parent you need to discuss boundaries, such as the student must maintain a C average and contribute say 20 percent of the cost of tuition to attend the school of their choice. By establishing the ground rules early and enforcing them, your child will be less likely to get in trouble and more likely to be the honor student you hoped for.

Finally, for those of you with the job promotion dilemma, sit down with the whole family and discuss the pros and cons of the opportunity and the move. It should be a family decision and not something you either dismiss out of hand or say yes to without consulting your family.

Yes, it is your career and you can see how this opportunity can yield huge dividends in your future with this company. However, you have a family and they need to be as excited about moving away from family and friends and starting over somewhere new as you are.

On the other hand, your family may surprise you by agreeing that moving to a new location would be fun and give you their blessing.

Remember this promotion is a big step for you but it is also a big step for them. You will have your company and the friends you made in the company to help you with the transition to the new location. Your family will not have any support system besides you when making the move.

I am not suggesting that you should let your family make the decision for you. Involving everyone in the process will ensure that everyone in the family feels good about the decision whether you decide to stay or to go. The dialogue may even lead to suggestions from your family on how to make the transition to the new location happen without incident or any hard feelings.

Remember, no one likes change. You will find that children, especially early teens, really hate changes that would force them to leave their friends. Do not dismiss this as childish behavior or you could find yourself dealing with a rebellious teenager. Make sure to talk through any and all advantages and disadvantages of making the move and listen to what they say about the move whether it is positive or negative.

If you don't have an immediate answer for a specific objection, don't say "Because I'm the parent that's why." Offer to research their objection, for example, "I am a good volleyball player and will get to play on the varsity team next year. It's not fair, I don't want to go." In this case, tell them that you don't know anything about the schools at the new location but to give you a week to talk to the people that work in that town and find out about the schools and after-school programs.

This should work with any objection they come up with. Doing the research will also help you decide whether this promotion is really the best choice for you and your family at this time.

Once you have all the facts, have another family meeting and review the additional pros and cons to accepting this promotion. At this point you should have enough information to make your decision and can discuss how things will change.

For those who decided to stay in town, now is the time to consider adding investments to your portfolio. I would suggest researching buying some rental real estate.

Some of you are saying, "but I don't want the hassle of people calling in the middle of the night because the toilet is overflowing." Others of you are concerned about people moving into the property and vandalizing it or burning it down.

A suggestion for finding and keeping good tenants is to have a clearly spelled out written agreement with each tenant that includes what items they are responsible for and which items you are responsible for. An example might be that tenants are responsible for any maintenance items under $50.00, this includes light bulbs, minor plumbing issues, such as dropping a spoon in the garbage disposal or a small leak. Anything major, such as the water heater or refrigerator stops working the tenant must call the homeowner/management company within 24 hours and allow access to assess and correct the issue. If after the assessment the repair costs under $50.00 then the tenant will pay the bill.

For those who consider themselves klutzes and unable to perform simple maintenance tasks, I suggest you research property management companies in your area. These companies charge a small percentage of the rental income to collect the rent checks, take tenants telephone calls, and fix maintenance issues. You also arrange with the management company what issues and the dollar amount that they are allowed to handle without your approval. Anything over that amount they must discuss with you prior to proceeding.

The trick with rental property is to make money. When doing your research on rental property keep in mind that the sales price is only a small part of the cost of owning a rental property. You are also responsible for taxes, insurance for the property, maintenance on the property, and, if you use a property management company, their fee.

After visiting a property and deciding it might work as an investment property, you should crunch the numbers to see if you will have a positive cash flow.

By this I mean, that when you add up your expenses, mortgage, insurance, 5-10 percent of the purchase price for maintenance (this is just a ballpark number to add to the equation), property management fee, and any other costs you may be expected to pay for, such as trash pickup, and subtract that number from the possible rental income, the result is a positive or negative amount.

> **Tip:** You may be able to get a list of expenses from the current owner to help you understand what is involved in keeping this property maintained.

If the number is negative, then this property is probably not a good investment for you. A positive number does not necessarily mean you should buy the property.

Once you decide to pursue a property, you need to conduct research on the neighborhood and the businesses near that neighborhood. When you buy your rental property, you want the property to be fully rented all the time. If the neighborhood is not close to businesses or commuter transportation, it may be harder to rent. Also, if the home is in a desirable neighborhood, it will command a higher rent.

To find out what properties rent for in a given neighborhood you can check with property management companies, internet research, or you can drive around an area and ask about properties with 'For Rent' signs in the yard.

Tip: Consider limiting your first rental property to the single family up to 4-family range. The reason for this is properties up to 4-family are considered residential for purposes of acquiring a mortgage.

Properties larger than 4-family are usually considered commercial which involves more paperwork and higher interest rates to acquire a mortgage.

More importantly your personal banker can help you apply for a residential loan. Often times he/she must send you to someone else to process a commercial loan

SUMMARY

This chapter discusses:

- Job opportunities and the advantages of being confident enough to handle increasingly responsible positions at work.
- Buying a new home due to increasing family size or moving to a new neighborhood.
- Researching and buying rental property.
- Finding a high school or college for your older children.

CHAPTER TWELVE

FIFTEEN YEARS LATER

"Everyone needs to strive for financial
freedom so that he or she can focus
on what he/she loves in life."

- **Todd M. Fleming**

Materials Required:

- Information on nursing homes (elderly parents or physically/mentally challenged children)
- 30 uninterrupted minutes

You have built a successful career with increasing salary and responsibilities. You have also bought a couple of rental properties in nice neighborhoods. These properties are always rented giving you a steady income stream each month.

Unfortunately, over the last couple of years it has become apparent that your elderly parents are no longer able to live alone. When you or your siblings visit, the house is a mess and worse it is clear your parents are not eating on a regular basis. You also realize they are not taking their medications as prescribed. When you ask about their eating habits and medications, they get confused by the questions or get angry.

You and your siblings have discussed various options from having your parents move into one of your homes to assisted living arrangements in their home vs. a nursing home.

Though this is a painful discussion, you are comforted to know that you can afford to send your parents to a well-respected nursing home, if that is deemed the appropriate solution for your parents.

Though your parents are resisting the idea of moving out of the home where they raised their children, you and your siblings convince them to let someone come in on a daily basis to check on them. The service you are hiring also includes help with cooking meals and housekeeping chores.

As a group you also let your parents know that if the service reports any instances where either they aren't allowed in the house or your parents seem to be acting irrationally, you will revisit the option of sending them to a nursing home.

It is an odd situation to be in, the children having to act as the parents but it must be done to ensure your parents' last days are comfortable and safe.

Some of you may have physically or mentally challenged children. As they get older you find they are taxing your abilities to take care of them at home. This is probably a more painful situation than dealing with elderly parents.

As with other situations you have dealt with, the key is to get all the facts. Go to the library; research the facilities available to treat your child's condition. Narrow down the choices and visit the ones that are on that list. Attend classes, visit the sleeping areas, talk with staff and other families while there and find out everything you can.

If you are considering in-home care, call the companies in your area that offer that service and interview anyone that might end up working for you. Do not just take the first person they send, interview them just like you would a prospective employee. You want someone your child will be comfortable with and who will treat your child with dignity and respect.

Remember their job is to help you take care of your child not to make your life more stressful.

For those of you who for various reasons have not bought a house or rental property, now would be a good time to review the chapters on home ownership and consider buying some real estate.

As mentioned earlier, real estate on average increases in value by 5 percent each year. Even if you had decided that credit mistakes you had made in the past made you ineligible for a mortgage, by now your steadily increasing income and fiscal responsibility makes you someone banks would consider lending money to.

I understand there are still some of you who feel that real estate is a big responsibility and that it ties you down. The point you are missing is that real estate also is one of the quickest ways to increase your investment value. And as for being tied down, if you like the area you are living in and the company you are working for, why not put down roots? Finally, for those of you who absolutely hate the thought of doing maintenance or yard work, I recommend condo living. Living in a condo is as close as you can get to apartment living with the added benefit of tax write-offs and appreciation.

Some of you at this point are reviewing options for working part-time or retiring from the workforce. This may be due to your being middle aged when you first picked up this book or it may be due to successful budgeting and planning on your part.

In either case, review your budget and calculate the result of employment and salary changes. If your salary decreases can you still pay your bills? It doesn't matter if the money comes from rental income, savings or other investment income.

If you see the amount due each month exceeds the amount of income you currently need to pay your bills, then you may need to consider a part-time position to make up the difference.

Don't feel that a part-time position is beneath you or worry over who would hire you at your age. Many companies are willing to hire seasoned workers for part-time positions. Retail operations from clothing stores to lumber yards are always looking for people to staff the off hours. They often want someone to work early hours like 6am to 10am or late hours like 6pm to 10pm to fill in around their full-time employees schedules.

These hours tend to work well for people who are looking for supplemental income from work that doesn't interfere with their ability to visit the doctor, get the car serviced and other activities that normally occur during the day.

SUMMARY

In this chapter, we discuss

- Expanding your rental property holdings.
- Finding a good nursing home or in-home care for aging parents.
- Transitioning to part time employment or even retiring.

CHAPTER THIRTEEN

TWENTY YEARS LATER

"Patience pays tons better than urge to get quick profit with same amount of investment."

- **Ankit Samrat**

Materials Required:

- Local College course list
- Blank paper
- 30 uninterrupted minutes

Many of you have followed the suggestions in this book and find yourself with positive cash flow from your rental property. Though you like the regular income and the appreciation found in real estate investing, you realize you need to diversify to ensure your wealth is always growing.

You have been reading a number of books on investment opportunities over the last few years and have decided to pursue stock investing.

You know that it can be riskier than investing in real estate, however; historically the stock market has earned a 10 percent return on investment.

To this end, you have subscribed to Investors Business Daily (IBD) and even took some classes at the local community college. One instructor was especially helpful in pointing out books to read, and as part of the class had everyone paper trading.

Note: There are also a lot of free resources on the internet that allow you to discover and review stock market opportunities.

Paper trading means research stocks, decide which stocks to buy and how many shares, but perform all transactions on paper only. You use the newspaper or the Internet to track the stock and get current prices, but have no actual money at risk. This gives you experience of trading stocks without worry. You can try different strategies, use different techniques and see if what you had been thinking would have worked in that situation.

Once you decide to actually start trading, start with a small amount of money.

The key to investing in the stock market is to make informed decisions, but if the market turns against you, you need to have a plan in place to either hold a stock through the downturn or to sell if it reaches a certain point. In either case, there is a potential for a loss and therefore stock market investing is something you should wait to start until you can afford to lose some, or all of your investment.

My personal philosophy on stock market investing is to always do your homework. If the stock is rock solid, based on your research, and there is a temporary downturn then I would stay in the stock. However, when the stock starts going down and I see some underlying change to the fundamental value of that stock, then I will sell if it drops 25 percent. This is called a stop loss position.

It means if I paid $20 for a stock and the stock drops to $15 and the underlying fundamentals that caused me to buy the stock in the first place have changed, then I will sell the stock.

Notice how this keeps emotion out of the equation? As long as I follow my own rules, in this case, the most I lose is $5 per share. If I get emotional about the stock and keep it because I like the product or the president or some other reason and do not look at the fundamentals, or worse ignore the fundamentals, I could lose the whole investment. Many good books explain stock market investing and I highly recommend you do plenty of research before jumping into the market.

SUMMARY

In this chapter you learned:

- How to research buying stocks and investing in the stock market.
- Using Paper trading to try out stock investing prior to trading using your own money.

CHAPTER FOURTEEN

TWENTY-FIVE YEARS LATER

"It is what a person will do with the saved money that will make a big difference in his or her finances"

- H. J. Chammas

A quarter of a century has passed since you first picked up this book. For some of you the early years were a struggle between scrimping and saving for a better tomorrow vs. temptation. Others just needed a road map. You knew that what you were doing was not working but did not know what to change or how to fix it.

It has been a long journey, but one you can look back on with pride and say, "I did it." Everyone said you would never amount to anything but look at you now.

You are independent, self-assured, and able to create a financial plan, stick with it and not let temptations sway you from what is important. Your goal was to be financially independent, to work if you wanted to work, not because you had to. You wanted to be able to go on vacation and still have income coming in, to leave for one to two months and know everything would be okay when you came back. And finally to teach your children money values so they too could become financially independent without having to take the road of hard knocks like you did.

Congratulations on your success. Though there are many other topics I would love to share with you, such as tax lien certificates, off shore real estate investing, cryptocurrency investing, it seems that now is a fitting time to end.

We have been together for twenty-five years. It has been a great time despite the early struggle and hard work and we are better people because of it.

We donate time and money to various charities and are respected members of our communities. We do what we want, when we want and live the life we always dreamed of.

Congratulations and thank you!

PART 2

MIRANDA'S STORY

"Millions wish for financial freedom, but only those that make it a priority have millions."

- Oscar Auliq-Ice

Today, I take control of my money!

One day at a time.

I can do this.

I am ready to change my life.

I can't live like this anymore! Time to get started.

This is an interesting book. I was expecting another boring financial book, but a friend told me it helped her get her finances in order and I decided to try it. The first step is to meditate.

Really? What does meditation have to do with managing my money?

Let me follow the instructions in Chapter One as I have never meditated before. Not sure what this has to do with managing money, yet the friends who told me about this book said just follow the steps and you will change your financial life. I really hope that's true.

Step 2—Get a small notebook and pen that will fit in my purse and carry it with me everywhere. I can do this. I'm going to keep reading the book to see what is coming up next. This tracking where my money is going seems too easy and I already know where it is going. Rent, gas for the car, water and sewer, electricity, food.

I promised myself I would give this a chance so I will spend the next two months listing all the money I receive and where it all goes. Not sure why I am doing this but it is my next step and I am going to follow the plan.

It's now two months later and I am actually seeing some things I am spending money on that maybe I shouldn't. Hmmm.

Step 3—Assemble the materials listed at the beginning of Chapter Three. Follow the instructions in Chapter Three regarding these materials. I can do this. The book suggests this first exercise will take 30 minutes to complete.

To get something different from my life, I must do something different. End of story. I bought this book because of the premise that following the instructions in this book could bring me financial freedom. I hope that is true. Please let it be true.

Financially free, not having to go to a 9-5 job anymore. Is that really what financial freedom means to me? Or is it more the ability to do what I want to when I want to regardless of what it costs?

Financial freedom is a great dream, but I am lucky to pay my bills each month. What was I thinking, buying a book that talks about becoming financially free? I bought it because I wanted to be the one who decides if I work for someone else or myself or just manage my investments and don't work at all.

I want this so badly. I promise to do the exercises and make the changes the book suggests.

I want a different life for my children than the one I had. This could be my way out. If I start before I have children they will never see how hard life can be. I can teach them how to save money and live the life they want right from the beginning. That would be incredible.

Raising financially independent children, what a concept. I remember how hard my life was. Lemonade stands, mowing the neighbors' yard, any odd job that I could get to make enough money to go to the movies or buy some candy.

Sometimes the money I received from odd jobs was used to pay for lunch at school. I know if I get out of this situation, my kids will laugh at me when I tell them about my childhood.

That's all right. As long as my children are healthy and respectful and don't grow up thinking money grows on trees, I'll be happy.

Label 6 envelopes. I can do that. I read the descriptions and understand what the envelopes stand for and why I need separate accounts. Financial freedom/retirement account seems so out of reach right now. I just need to trust that over time the changes I make now will make a difference.

Help me, Great Spirit, make the right choices.

I am weak and fear that I will screw this up.

I always make a mess of things.

I want to be good.

I want to be the one everyone at the class reunion wishes they were.

Two envelopes are all I need to concentrate on right now. I can follow these instructions. I will follow these instructions. It is my life and it will be better starting today!

If I make a mistake, I will try again.

I will not give up!

Winners sometimes lose, but winners Never give up!

I know this book is about finances, but maybe I should start thinking about my long-term goals. Where did that thought come from?

I know things won't change overnight but maybe now is a good time to start thinking about the future.

I'm sure that in the next chapter, we'll be doing something with that envelope labeled long-term saving for spending and that definitely has something to do with the future.

What do I want to save for? Am I saving for a new car, a down payment on a house? Well as long as I'm dreaming, how about one of those trips around the world I keep seeing advertised on TV?

Hmmm…Why not? Why shouldn't I dream big? I deserve it. I read somewhere that knowing what you want and focusing on achieving that goal gets you halfway to reaching it. At the time I just thought that was a bunch of hooey by some hoity-toity psychology professor. But what if I'm wrong?

Maybe there is something to this goal setting and believing in what you are doing. I have already made a commitment to myself to read this book and follow the suggestions contained within. I've even labeled 6 envelopes and read the first two chapters.

I recognize this book was not custom written for me. It may contain information that is not applicable to my situation. Furthermore, because this book is not written by someone licensed as a financial advisor any material contained within should be run past my own financial advisor or tax accountant to ensure what I am doing is appropriate for my circumstances.

Tax accountant, financial advisor—why not a lawyer and personal banker? Boy, when I get carried away with an idea it really gets pretty wild.

Me, the "Queen of living for today," suggesting I have a list of financial professionals to discuss my circumstances with.

Negative thoughts—be gone!

I promise to do whatever I need to: Ignore/quash/redirect any negative thoughts, and if possible turn them into positive results instead.

I will no longer let my unconscious mind take me out of the money game!

My life is too important to let negativity from myself or others keep me from reaching my financial goals.

So far, I have been meditating daily and completed the first exercise. I am looking forward to continuing on this road of financial discovery.

Budget forms, expenses vs. income, math problems... Oh, no! I can't do math. I flunked out of several math classes over the years. The teachers told me I was hopeless and should consider finding a husband to take care of me, because I wouldn't be able to take care of myself.

What should I do? I guess I should give up right now. I'll never fill the form out correctly. This just isn't for me.

Well, I guess I could use a calculator to help with any math problems I need to solve in this chapter. It's not like school, where the teacher expects you to solve problems without a calculator and show your work. Maybe this budgeting thing won't be so hard. What good is a budget in my circumstances?

Money comes in, pays bills; then, the end of the month comes. Money is all gone.

I already know this.

Wait! What am I saying? I am only at Chapter Four. I promised myself I would give this book a chance. The author stated that following the instructions in this book would change my financial life. I have some evidence of that already.

Okay, I've got to pull myself together. I already decided to get the negativity out of my life. You, (devil on the shoulder—naysayer—stay where you are, it's safe there) my negative little voice, are not going to stop me from completing this exercise.

I have had issues with math in the past. This is true. However, I also had many successes, mainly due to supportive teachers who stayed late and helped me learn the material. It is not that I'm stupid, I took one of those standardized tests once and they said my IQ was 135. That really didn't mean much to me, but according to the paperwork that accompanied the test results, 135 is borderline genius.

That's a kick in the pants. I'm almost a genius but I have trouble with math. Imagine that! Anyway, the first teacher that helped me with the mathematical concepts realized that part of my problem was my eyesight.

It turned out I was farsighted, which meantI needed eyeglasses or contacts to read things that are close. It was puzzling at first why I was doing well in reading class until I realized I always checked out books that had large print.

Well, enough of that trip down memory lane! See, there is no reason to get stressed over doing some simple math problems. Besides, the list of items necessary to complete this chapter includes a calculator.

FINANCIAL FREEDOM

"Freedom comes when you're Brave Enough
to chase your dreams, and achieve the
Success and Financial Freedom you want.

In order to be FREE, you have to be BRAVE."

- Jeanette Coron

As long as the word problems are clearly described, and I have a calculator handy to check my work, I can complete this section.

Okay, time to pull out the sample budget, and a blank budget form, and get started.

List of my income and where it comes from. Well, that's pretty easy. I am a typist/receptionist at the XYZ Co. earning $15.00 per hour. I get paid weekly, so I guess I can multiply by 4 to get my monthly totals, but I think it works better for my circumstances if I instead change the budget form to show income on a weekly basis.

I've now filled in the top line of the budget form to correspond to the date of each paycheck. I have even filled in my take home pay for the next 4 weeks.

Next I work on my bills. I think the best way to do this is to first sort them by due date and then list them by due date on the budget form.

Rent will be the first item under the expense category. I will put the dollar amount for rent, $750 per month for my share of the rent, under the paycheck that will fall closest to the first of each month. In some months this will correspond to the last paycheck of the previous month. The last thing I want to be is late with the rent and find myself out on the street.

I will list the rent for the remainder of the year, as it won't change until my anniversary date. It didn't change last year, but I heard some rumors around the apartment complex that the rent will be going up this year.

I may have to look for a new place to live if that happens. I can barely afford to live here now, but it is a nice place to live. I love the neighborhood, the proximity to shopping and restaurants mean I can walk everywhere, reducing the wear and tear on my 10-year-old car.

The next bills are various credit cards, again sorted by due date. I added a couple of columns to the sample budget. One column is for the due date to help me spot when bills are due and the other is a total amount owed, which shows me how much total debt I have outstanding.

Right now the amount of debt I am carrying on credit cards is pretty disheartening. The credit card interest rates are staggering. I know I have to get out from under this mountain of debt, but how?

Take a deep breath! Yes, things look bleak right now but remember; it is always darkest before dawn. I have taken the first step to improving things.

I realized, after listing money flows in the small notebook in Chapter Two, that I had been going to a lot of lunches with folks from work, and that money could be better spent on paying down the credit card bills.

I budgeted going to lunch with my team once a month. I don't want to appear antisocial, but I know that unless I show some restraint now, I won't be able to achieve my long-term goals.

Did I really say that? Me, "Miss live for today" saying I need to practice restraint? No more running to the store to buy something/anything just because I had a bad day at work, or because the car wouldn't start, or Mary Lou was mean to me.

Putting all this mess on paper and tracking it is the first step to fixing what's wrong. I have always been a visual person, if I can't see it, or at least visualize it, it's as if it didn't exist. I've heard other people say that they need to hear something in order to assimilate the information.

I guess that's what makes us all unique individuals. Anyway, back to my budget. Now that I've got all my income and expenses listed in the budget, it's time to review the envelopes.

Oh, NO! Not only is there more math but I also need to work with percentages!

Self, calm down. It's okay. Look, the section that talks about how to split the percentages into the various envelopes also shows a very detailed description of how the author came up with the numbers.

Percentages. It's about splitting something into pieces. I remember now, the teacher used an example of cutting a round pie into pie shaped parts and another teacher used a rectangle representing a piece of fabric to show real life examples of using percentages.

I see in the examples how the author shows step by step the way the percentages look when I am working with my ideal budget and an example of what my budget might look like right now.

I have been thinking about my long-term goals for a while now and have decided going to college and buying a new car are the two goals I want to work on right now.

After putting together the income and expense part of my budget, I realize that I am only able to put aside $3.00 per paycheck toward all non-necessity goals. This means I will be putting sixty-seven cents toward each of the following categories: fun, retirement/financial freedom, long-term savings and education, while thirty-two cents will go into the envelope labeled charity.

I decided to add another line item on my budget for 401k contributions, because I am currently putting 2 percent of my gross income into the company 401k plan. The really unexpected result is, as the author said, it had no effect on my take home pay. I still don't understand the tax implications, and why this worked out this way, but I guess I don't have to. Some things you just need to do on faith.

I know that technically the 401k contributions should be included in the RET envelope. However, at this point, doing that would skew the results unfairly.

I want to not only be able to see my money accumulating, but to be able to know exactly where it is. Unless I split out everything into individual line items, it will be harder for me to see at a glance where my money is, and how it is doing.

I have been putting sixty-seven cents in the envelopes labeled RET and FUN and even spent the money from the FUN account on something frivolous.

It was hard to do that, but the book keeps talking about keeping the inner child happy to prevent sabotaging your financial plans.

The funny thing is, I am less stressed about money now than I was before I bought this book. How can that be?

Nothing has really changed. My life still sucks.

My bills are still higher than my income most months, but I can see how following the instructions in this book may get me out of my current situation.

I promised myself I would try something new and not second-guess the book or myself. I chose this book and I will stick with it until the end. Maybe it will work.

Out! Out, I say! How many times do I have to banish you, you negative thought!

I won't let you sabotage my efforts any longer!

I am better than this! I am a money magnet and am worthy of wealth and happiness!

I have money in a 401k account. Who would have thought?

When I bought this book, I was thinking how hopeless my life was. I was looking at people around me, and wishing I was anyone but me.

Now, I am feeling better about my life. I can see there is a lot of hard work ahead but I know I can do it.

Look what I accomplished so far. I have signed up for the company 401k plan. I am putting 2 percent of my income into the account, and just got my first statement. I made 5 cents on my contribution. WOW!

I bought a piece of Bazooka bubble gum using the money in my FUN account. It was a struggle to spend the money that way as I have this mountain of bills to pay, but after buying it, unwrapping the gum, and reading the comic inside, I actually felt less stressed. I can't explain it, except to say that there is something to that FUN account.

I don't know why this is working, or if it really will make me financially independent, but I am going to continue reading the book and see what happens next.

Surprisingly, setting up the budget wasn't so hard. I used the blank form in the back of the book. I probably shouldn't have used the Xerox machine at work to make copies, but everyone else does it.

Yes, mom, I hear you, "If everyone else was jumping off the bridge would you follow them?"

I know how you feel about my following the crowd especially if it means doing something that is ethically or morally wrong.

I just wanted to get started as soon as possible and getting to the Kinko's or the library to make copies wasn't happening soon enough. So I made copies and am dealing with my conscience regarding using the company resources.

I have posted my budget on the wall in my home office. I am finding the visual representation of my bills is helping me stay on track.

Wow! Four months of reading this book and following the suggestions, and I am saving money. I know where my money is going, and I am looking forward to the future. Who would have thought that possible? One book– one little book–could be so life changing. I can't wait to see what the other chapters suggest I do.

I am starting to think differently about money. It's no longer something I don't have enough of, and wish I had more of. It is now something I track. Something I plan for. I understand that if I spend money on something that is not on the budget already, I may have trouble paying my bills later in the year. That is such a revelation! It sounds so simple and trite, but since starting down this road I have learned that just because something looks simple and easy, doesn't mean that it is easy to do consistently.

However, seeing how a Mocha Grande from Starbucks, which is not on the budget, impacts what I can save in the retirement or long-term goal envelopes, helps keep me on track. Also, receiving those quarterly statements from the company 401k plan that show my contributions, dividends and interest accruing in the account, really proves that this works.

As I need reminders of what I am doing, and why, I have also hung photographs of a new car and a college diploma on the wall next to the budget and 401k statements.

The money going into the envelopes doesn't look like much now, but I posted that table showing how one penny doubled 30 times becomes $5 million. I don't want $5,000,000. I'm not sure I want $100,000, however starting with $0.67 a week I can see how that can grow into something sizable, if I just let it. I just have to have faith, follow the plan, and everything will turn out all right.

I have been doing research in the library. It's amazing how many kinds of jobs are out there. Many of them say you need a college degree, but there are still plenty of opportunities for those of us with high school diplomas. I did some research on the company I currently work for to find out what other types of jobs they have and discovered we are a small division of a multinational corporation.

Why didn't anyone ever tell us that? That information is important to me and probably is to a lot of other people in our division. It shows I can go places with this company. I don't have to leave this company to achieve my long-term goals.

It looks like I might have to move to a different state to keep growing with this company, but that's okay. I was looking at the bulletin board out-side the Human Resources (HR) department and saw an opening for a reconciliation clerk in the accounting department. Maybe I can talk to someone in the HR department and see what I need to do to apply for that position.

I was reading about accounting positions in the occupational handbook the government puts out and from what I've read, I think I am qualified to do that job.

I think I will talk to HR first, so I know what the procedure is to transfer to another department. I know my boss likes my work, but I don't see myself as a receptionist/typist for the rest of my career.

While I was at the library, I researched college classes. They even have some free seminars on financial topics coming up soon. I seem to remember my company offering financial assistance to people going to college. When I am in the HR office I'm going to check into that. Maybe I can take some night classes, so I can learn some concepts used in the accounting department.

If I play my cards right, I may be able to get transferred to the corporate accounting division in a couple of years. I think I'd like to live in Denver for a while. Well, I better slow down; make some notes on college courses, registration information, free seminar dates, times, and what the job guide says a reconciliation clerk does. Then I'll talk to someone in the HR department.

YIPEE! I spoke with HR about college courses, and the open position in the accounting department. Gayle told me that the company would pay 100 percent of my tuition, provided I earn a grade of an A or B.

They will pay 75 percent of the tuition for a C and nothing if I receive anything less than a C. She told me that I needed to pay for the class up front and then the company will reimburse me when I bring in my report card as proof of completion and final grade.

I just missed the start of the fall semester, so I have 3 months to save up for the spring semester, or almost a year to save up for next fall. I am going to the local college tonight after work and get a current schedule of classes and prerequisites.

I'm going to college!

I also found out that the reconciliation clerk position had been filled, but the HR person told me there are a couple of other positions that I might find interesting. We discussed the positions the person in HR thought I might be qualified for and I left to think about everything I learned in the last couple of days.

It's incredible. I have gone to the college and signed up for the introductory accounting class. The woman in the registrar's office told me that I will need to take Freshman English class and two philosophy classes to graduate, but agreed to let me start with the accounting class. Because classes won't be starting for another three months, the registrar said I wouldn't be required to pay for class until 15 days prior to the start of the class.

This is a good thing because I have only accumulated $2.01 toward that goal. I realize that even 3 months from now I will only have $4.02 in the education envelope and will need to put my class tuition on a credit card.

BUDGETS ARE POWER

"The analysation of your spending habits
is key to your financial success"

- Neala Okuromade

Though I hate the thought of putting more debt on a credit card, I also realize that maintaining at least a B average will lead to my being reimbursed the full amount of the class in approximately four months time.

Also, unlike other reasons I have added to my credit card debt, taking college classes gets me closer to my goal. I can move out of the receptionist/typist position, and into a professional position.

So far I have spoken to Gayle in the HR department about openings in the accounting department, but they are looking for someone with experience, or at least some college courses.

When I mentioned I had signed up for an accounting class, Gayle encouraged me. She said I have a much better chance of at least getting an interview the next time the accounting department has an opening for a junior level person.

My class starts in 3 months on Monday and Wednesday nights and lasts for 12 weeks. I have bought the textbook and started reading the first couple of chapters.

The terms are a bit confusing, debit and credit for example; I think they have to do with what side of the balance sheet the number is on, but what does that mean? Well that's just one of many questions I have for the instructor. I am really looking forward to learning new things and climbing that next rung on the corporate ladder.

I have been so busy working on paying off my credit card debt, looking into college classes that I can afford, and talking to HR about other opportunities at work, that I lost track of the fact that I am 50 days away from my rental anniversary date. It turns out the rumors are true. I just came home and found a letter from the landlord. My rent is going up 10 percent starting on my anniversary date.

A 10 percent increase means my rent will be $825 a month starting in less than 2 months. Do I look like I'm made of money?

No need to panic. I saw something in the book that talks about home ownership. I am probably jumping the gun. Me, owning my own home, that's pretty far fetched.

But, only a few months ago if someone had told me I would be contributing money to the company 401k plan and creating a budget that I actually used, I'd have told them they were crazy.

So let's get started and review my options.

- **Advantages of home ownership**: It's mine. I may get a tax deduction and within certain limits, I can do whatever I want there.
- **Advantages to renting**: If anything goes wrong, it is not my problem. I just pay my rent to live there. Anything that happens with the property is someone else's responsibility.

Financially, renting vs. buying means I need to come up with a security deposit or a down payment, respectively. In both cases I have to make a monthly payment either to the landlord in the form of rent, or the mortgage company to pay for my new home.

Renting I usually sign a one-year lease, whereas with buying a home you sign a fifteen or thirty-year mortgage.

Usually the only check the rental company does, before allowing me to rent an apartment, is to confirm I pay my bills on time, particularly rent, and that my take home pay is enough to pay the rent. A mortgage company wants to be sure that I am not overburdening myself. They limit how much of my income can be spent on my loan payments.

This means that credit card debt plus mortgage amount are added together and compared to the bank's ideal percentage of total debt divided into total income before the bank agrees to loan me the money.

After I review the options on renting vs. buying a home, I realize that I need to pay down my credit card debt before I can get a bank to loan me money for a mortgage.

KNOW THYSELF

"Pay your bills, yes. But don't invest
in them. Invest in your dreams.
What you invest in grows."

- Suzette Hinton

I know I need to do something to reduce my credit card debt but am not sure where to start. I decided to jump to Appendix C and read the section on how to pay for emergencies. In that section the author talks about using something called an unsecured loan instead of credit cards.

I don't have a personal banker or even a regular bank branch, but I think it's time I found one. I have a checking account at a local bank, so I guess I'll start there and ask about an unsecured loan.

I went to the bank at lunch today and discovered they were willing to approve me for a $2,000 unsecured loan. It had a low interest rate and a repayment period of three years. I signed the paperwork, and they deposited the money into my checking account.

I can't believe it. The loan officer said that they offer bank customers with regular jobs unsecured loans with values up to 10 percent of their salary. This is really useful information. I wish I knew it before I got so far in debt with the credit card companies. The interest rate is much less than I pay on my credit cards, and I can pay off the loan much sooner because more of the payment goes towards paying down the principal.

I also mentioned that my long-term goal was owning my own home, and the loan officer assured me that paying my loan and credit card payments on time would help make that possible. He even went over some ratios the bank uses to decide how much moneyI could qualify for.

I thanked him for his time and asked for his business card. He said I could call any time if I had any other questions regarding different types of loans.

Does this mean I now have a personal banker? Well, maybe that is jumping the gun a bit, but at least I have a relationship with someone at a bank who can answer my questions.

After our conversation, I realized that as much as I hate to move, and as much as I like my current apartment, I really need to reduce my expenses.

One way to do that is to look for a cheaper apartment, as my rent is going to increase $75 per month in less than two months.

While researching what is available to rent I found a beautiful apartment down the street from where I live now. It is one half of an older duplex and includes a one-car garage.

BUY IT RIGHT

"The first way to save and invest your money is to have a budget, and it should be prepared when you have absolutely nothing. Once the funds have gone into your account, start keeping a record of every expenditure, and don't go for things which are not in the budget. Compare the budget and actual in the following month."

- Ekare

The added benefit is that instead of paying $75 more per month for the apartment I am currently living in, I will end up paying $50 less per month, which I split between my long-term goals of a new car, college, and down payment. Though a down payment was not in the original budget, it was more because I didn't believe I could ever save enough to own a home rather than not wanting my own home.

Living off a budget has had some unexpected benefits. I have discovered that more things are possible. I applied for and was approved for an unsecured loan. I have updated my budget to include a line item for a down payment on a house. I have contributed 2 percent of my income into the company 401k plan for several months now.

And when I moved into my new apartment, I learned that the people that live next door are actually the owners. I have been talking to them about real estate and how they got started and I am feeling a lot more confident in my ability to do what they are doing someday.

I also started dating a guy I met in the accounting program at college. It's still a new relationship but we've had a few conversations on his views of money and finances. I don't want to scare him off but I want him to know that I understand budgeting and saving for long-term goals and plan on being involved in the finances should our relationship become more serious.

He seems to understand where I am coming from and is willing to be partners in financial matters.

It's pretty amazing. I have successfully completed two college classes toward my accounting degree. I still haven't decided if I am just going to stop taking classes after completing the accounting certificate program or if I am going to stay in school until I attain a Bachelor's degree. I have a 4.0 grade point average (all As), and so far my company has paid all the costs of my education.

I just interviewed for a clerk position in the accounting department. My college courses helped get me the interview. They were impressed with the annual reviews in my personnel file, my knowledge of what the department does, and what the position requires. I am hopeful that they will select me to fill that opening.

I have also been reading the classified section of the paper looking for real estate opportunities. I have learned there are certain phrases, like, "Owner moving out of town", "Must sell", "For sale by owner", that means a property seller is flexible. This often means that they may accept a lower sales price or offer you the opportunity to pay them for the property over time rather than make you get a mortgage from a bank.

I have circled some ads. I even drove around town looking at some properties that I circled in the paper, but so far I haven't found anything that I would pay to live in. My neighbors have also shown me how to look for real estate opportunities online to get quicker and more timely ads to review.

Good news! I got the clerk position! My boss is sad to lose a valuable employee, but we have discussed my career plans and he is very supportive.

I will be transitioning to my new department next week.

It's hard to believe, I'm going to be working in the accounting department!

Oh No! I don't know what I was thinking. I had a simple assignment: answer the telephone and handle the occasional typing assignment. Now I'm going to work as a clerk in the accounting department.

It's happening again. My negative voices are trying to stop me.

I am so close. I can do this!

I know how to learn new things.

One day at a time. Ask lots of questions.

Take Notes.

Make a To-Do-List.

Go over it with the Boss.

Find out what is most important to the boss.

In the beginning no one expects you to know everything. Don't pretend like I know everything. Ask for help! Remember, questions are expected of the new hire.

I have never done this job before and they know it. They still hired me for the job. So relax, breathe, and follow instructions.

I can do this! I know I can! I'm attending college and maintaining a 4.0 Grade Point Average (GPA). I have a new position at work partly due to my college courses and GPA.

This is what I have been working toward for the last year.

I will not sabotage my efforts!

I believe in myself and will prove to everyone that I am the right candidate for this position.

I have survived the first week! I am feeling more confident in my ability to handle this position. I follow instructions and ask a question when something is unclear.

I have banished the negative voices but for how long? Will I have to battle the negativity every time I try something new?

Stop it! I promised myself I would take it one day at a time; follow my plan and not second-guess myself.

Look how much I have accomplished so far, college classes, a new job, a new apartment, long-term relationship with a bank.

I am learning about real estate investing from someone that has done it. I am reading the classified ads in the newspaper and looking for key phrases. I am driving around the various neighborhoods looking at property that is for sale and getting a feel for what things cost.

This is fun. I can't wait until I can afford to buy a home of my own.

What a difference a couple of years make! John and I got married last week. He's the guy I met in the accounting program at school.

I just received a great annual review and a substantial raise with added responsibilities. Part of the increase is due to graduating from the certificate program with a 4.0 GPA (grade point average).

All that research has paid off. John and I are about to make an offer on our first house. While we were dating, I showed him this book and suggested he start a budget, and use the envelopes.

NOW IS THE RIGHT TIME

"The secret of financial breakthroughs:
Pay ten percent of any income you receive
to God(tithe)and save ten percent of your
income as a payment for yourself."

- Lailah Gifty Akita

He agreed, and we now have a substantial down payment and are buying a triplex. We will live in one unit and rent out the other two units. I have learned a lot from my current landlord about renting property to others and have spoken to their lawyer to ensure John and my rights are protected.

My banker has been instrumental in getting us a very competitive fixed-rate mortgage. The sellers were moving out-of-town due to a job change and were willing to lower the price for a quick sale.

When I saw the property, I knew that this was the one. It is in a good neighborhood, near shopping and a number of businesses, and is in very good condition.

We wrote up a contract offering them 90 percent of the sales price with contingencies for a termite inspection, structural review (the building was built in the 1950s), and a general building inspection. I specified that all items currently in the three units transfer with the units. This included not only the window treatments and installed lighting fixtures, but furniture and rugs in the units and the lawn equipment in the storage shed.

I also had a contingency to ensure that I wouldn't have to buy the house if I was unable to secure a mortgage on the property. We agreed to a closing date in 90 days to make sure I could get everything done in time.

I fully expected a counter offer from the owners, but they accepted my offer. That meant I had to mobilize the resources necessary to check out the property and confirm my gut feeling was accurate.

Everyone that checked out the building agreed that it was structurally sound and a good deal. When the bank had the property appraised, they found that the property was worth $30,000 more than what I agreed to pay for the property.

What a great way to start a new life.

After John and I bought the triplex, we decided to use ACME Property Management Company to handle the two rental units. Though we are both mechanically inclined, we realize that there are more important things we could be doing with our time than managing tenants and toilets.

We tell the management company not to tell the renters that we are the owners. We live next door to them and want to just be neighbors. This lets us keep an eye on the property without confrontation. So far, the tenants have been conscientious, friendly people who we enjoy having as friends and neighbors.

We have a new income stream. Most of the boxes are unpacked from the move. The "Thank You" notes for our wedding presents are in the mail. Now it's time to consider creating a joint budget.

We assemble all our bills, our sources of income, and our current budgets. We sit down with a blank budget form and brainstorm our long-term goals.

While brainstorming, we jointly decided our long-term goals include: buying more rental properties, investing in the stock market, and precious metal and/or gemstone investing.

This led to the following long-term plan:

> 5% current income—rental property
>
> 3% current income—stock market investing
>
> 2% current income—precious metals/gemstones

We next reviewed 401k contributions and decided to increase our contributions to 7 percent of our current salary.

To help clarify our goals, we listed real estate investing classes and stock market investing seminars on the education envelope.

Our only heated discussion occurred over the charitable contributions. I have strong feelings about donating to the American Heart Association and the American Diabetes Organization, while John feels that most charitable organizations spend too much on overhead and not enough on helping people.

He instead donates time and money to the Habitat for Humanity program because he can see the results.

In the end, we agree to a compromise. We will send half of our charitable contribution to the organizations I support and half to the organizations John supports.

This leads to three envelopes to hold our charitable contributions (5 percent of current income):

1.5% of current income—American Heart Association

1% of current income—American Diabetes Organization

2.5% of current income—Habitat for Humanity

We also realized that a combined FUN account would not work for us. So instead, we created his and her envelopes and put one-half of the total amount into each envelope.

Some months, we decide to use the money in the FUN account to do something fun together, like a weekend getaway in the mountains, but most months we spend the money on something we want individually.

I usually go to the day spa and have a massage and a manicure while John goes to the woodworking store, and either buys more tools or takes a class. He's actually gotten pretty good at making dowels and is now working on creating chairs and using the dowels as supports for the back and arms of the chairs.

It's a good thing the triplex has a detached 2-car garage, because John has so much wood and equipment we wouldn't have any place to park the car if we only had a 1-car garage.

Another year has gone by. Because I haven't been feeling well the last couple of days, I went to see the doctor. He ran some tests and just called to tell me that I'm pregnant. I share the news with John when he gets home and John is ecstatic.

I guess I can make the announcement at the anniversary party our friends are holding for us tonight at our favorite restaurant.

The other good news is that our rental property is yielding an extra $300 per month income, which we had earmarked for a down payment on additional rental property.

Now that I am pregnant John and I will need to revisit our long-term goals to include new expenses related to child-care and the child's education. But, tonight we celebrate our four-year anniversary and revel in the good news.

As we are getting ready to go to the party, our real estate agent, Paul, calls. He says he just signed a listing with a very motivated seller and thought we might be interested in the property.

It is a fully rented duplex in a desirable neighborhood. The seller is willing to hold the mortgage with a 5 percent down payment. Paul gives me an overview of the deal and offers to fax over the details after we hang up. I mentioned that John and I are celebrating our four year anniversary tonight so we won't have a chance to talk about the deal until tomorrow. Paul says in his opinion the property is underpriced and should sell quickly so we shouldn't wait too long to make a decision.

KEEP UP THE GOOD WORK!

"Financial fitness is not a pipe dream or
a state of mind. It's a reality if you are
willing to pursue it and embrace it."

- Will Robinson

I glance at the wall where our budget is posted and realize that we have enough money in the down payment account to buy this property. Once Paul sends over the details, John and I can sit down and discuss if now is the right time to add another property to our portfolio.

For now, we need to leave in order to get to the restaurant on time for our anniversary party. After dinner, I announced my pregnancy. I received some of the strangest reactions to the announcement. People I thought would be happy for us were the most vocal as to how having a child was the worst thing that could happen to you. They brought up sleepless nights while the child is a baby, then the cost of college, the list of reasons seemed endless. The funny thing was the most vocal were also the ones that did not have any children. So everything they said was at best anecdotal based on other friends and family members' situations.

I decided to ignore their negativity, just as I did years earlier when I first started using this financial system.

John and I are ecstatic about this pregnancy and will do whatever it takes to ensure this child is loved and cared for.

When John and I return home, I find the fax from Paul waiting for us. I grab the fax as I tell John about the conversation with Paul. We pull the budget off the wall, get some blank paper, pencil, and calculator and sit down at the kitchen table to crunch some numbers.

We see from the comparables that this property is listed at $10,000 less than the average sales price in that neighborhood. We also see that average rents for apartments in that neighborhood are higher than the current rents being paid by the tenants.

We agree this looks promising, but want to see the neighborhood and the property before committing to the deal. I call Paul and ask him to set up an appointment to see the property.

The next morning, I called my personal banker and asked him about mortgage options. It is tempting to accept the owner financed option, but I felt we would be in a stronger bargaining position if I had other financing options to consider.

Paul was able to arrange a visit to the property at noon. As John and I are both working, we drive separately to the duplex and meet Paul there rather than going to his office first. We find the exterior is in poor condition; bushes and trees are overgrown and some of them could be considered hazardous.

What little paint is left on the house is peeling and some areas without paint, especially around the windowsills, look rotten.

John and I look at each other and are tempted to say we've seen enough, but decide that as long as we are here, we might as well go inside.

As distressing as the outside is, the inside is immaculate. Everything in both units is pristine. There is fresh paint on the walls. The appliances are fairly new and work well. Decorative light fixtures and window treatments add to the desirability of the units.

We meet one of the tenants coming home for lunch and ask about the building and the current landlord. The tenant says he's lived in the building for 5 years and the landlord used to have someone take care of the grounds. He's not sure what happened, but he hasn't seen anyone regularly perform yard work in a couple of years.

However, as part of his lease, he is responsible for maintaining the interior of the building. If he decides to do anything structural, such as moving a wall or installing a closet he needs the landlord's approval. Otherwise, he can do what he feels needs to be done on the inside.

The tenant also mentions it's a great neighborhood to live in, and he plans to stay, assuming the new owner wants tenants. He points out a number of homes in the area that the new owners changed from duplex to single family homes. He says he hopes the new owners will keep this building a rental.

John and I thank him for his candor and tell Paul we will give him our decision by 8 pm that evening. John and I return to work, but I keep thinking about the duplex and crunching numbers in my head.

That night, while I am preparing dinner, John and I discuss the pros and cons of the duplex. We review all the deferred maintenance items. We then call Paul and tell him what we want to do.

He comes over and we jointly write up the offer for the property.

I am interested in using owner financing for this deal but I am not willing to pay more in interest than I would pay if I took a mortgage on the property from the bank. I have Paul include a clause in the contract that says we will accept owner financing, if the owner will agree to a 6 percent fixed interest rate for 30 years with a no prepayment penalty clause.

I know this is reasonable. I talked to my banker and he told me he could loan the money for this property at 6 percent for 30 years with no prepayment clause. The main reason I am interested in using owner financing is there is no loan application and no ratios that I must satisfy to justify the loan.

CHILDREN NEED BUDGETS TOO

"Who you are tomorrow begins
with what you do today."

- Tim Fargo

Two hours later, Paul calls us with the owner's answer. The owner acknowledged the deferred maintenance items and agreed to pay for tree and shrub trimming and/or removal and lawn maintenance. He agreed to a 30 year 6 percent interest loan with a 5 percent down payment, but increased the sales price I had offered him by $5,000. He also asked for a closing in 5 days from acceptance.

I had offered 15 percent less than the owner's original offer. John and I had crunched the numbers using the original sales price and saw that even at full price the property would generate a positive cash flow. I agree to the counter offer.

I ask that one final statement be inserted into the document: If all the deferred maintenance items that the owner agreed to handle were not completed by the closing, then $10,000 of the sales proceeds would be held in escrow until the work was completed. This amount would come out of our down payment.

All sides agree and the closing is set.

At closing, all items had been resolved so the previous owner left with his proceeds. John and I leave with ownership of the duplex and receive the information on where to send our loan payments. We then stop by the duplex and introduce ourselves to the tenants. We are so excited to start this new adventure.

We explain that we are the new owners and that we want a smooth transition. We received copies of their current lease agreements at closing and confirmed with each tenant the contents are accurate. We also confirm that each tenant wants to continue their lease.

We give them the information on where to send their rent checks, and the phone number of the management office should they have any problems. We also ask for their opinion on any items that they feel need immediate attention.

The consensus was the lack of regular yard work and painting the exterior of the building were the two biggest problems they had with the previous landlord.

We thank them for their time and leave to review the list of maintenance items still needing completion.

After a number of contractors reviewed the exterior of the duplex and returned estimates greater than 25 percent of our purchase price for the property, John and I decided to call some aluminum siding contractors for an estimate.

A month after the purchase of the duplex

A number of the aluminum siding contractors suggested just removing the obviously rotten wood, then siding over the rest without much prep work. Granted, the cost was very reasonable, but we had concerns about how well the building would age if we followed those suggestions.

After doing some more research on aluminum siding contractors, we decided to use a man that our neighbor recommended. He was reputable, licensed, bonded, and insured. More importantly, he sat down with John and me and explained exactly what needed to be done.

Though his estimate was not the cheapest, it was the most comprehensive, and included a twenty-year warranty on all work.

John and I had hopes of returning the building to its original glory, but realized that it was not practical or cost effective and agreed to the aluminum siding.

Then a really strange thing began to happen. After the aluminum siding project was completed on our duplex, neighbors around our duplex started painting their homes, cleaning up their yards, trimming hedges and planting flowers.

Three months after the purchase of the duplex

If I hadn't seen it with my own eyes I would never have believed that one person could make a change in the way a neighborhood looked or acted.

Five months later

Today's the big day. I've been in labor for hours and June has finally decided to grace us with her presence. She is a healthy, 8-pound 2 ounce bundle of joy. The doctor wants to keep us overnight for observation but assuming there are no complications, we will be home tomorrow.

The duplex John and I bought nine months ago has turned out better than expected. We were reviewing the survey that was included with the closing documents and discovered we owned an empty lot next to the lot the duplex sits on.

We've been researching zoning regulations in the neighborhood and now know that we can build another duplex on the vacant lot or we could combine the two lots and build a 6-plex (this anomaly is due to a grandfather clause).

If we choose the quick cash option, we can sell the vacant lot for almost as much as we paid for the whole property. Conversely, if we go with building a duplex on the other lot or even adding a four plex across the two lots, we could substantially increase our rental income. This option would require cash to pay the builder thus decreasing our ability to save for a while.

So many options! It is amazing how well things are turning out. Someone once said that if you open yourself up to the universe good things would come to you. I didn't know what that meant, or even believed that good things could happen to me, but then I found this book. I followed the steps, which included writing words on envelopes, creating a budget, and putting money in envelopes based on what the budget said.

The steps were so deceptively simple and yet so powerful. Instead of still being a receptionist/typist making just enough to get by, I work in the accounting department and have a college diploma on my wall. I own my own home and have rental property as well. I am well on my way to my dream life with the man I love and a new baby.

3 months after June is born

Today is our five-year anniversary. We have a 3-month-old and we've decided to celebrate with a quiet evening at home. Our four rental units are adding an extra $750 per month to our household income.

I took maternity leave from my job when June was born, but tomorrow it ends and I'll be going back to work. While on leave, I researched day care options and found a great pre-school program for June. They accept children from newborns to 5-year-olds. If this program works out, I won't have to worry about finding June a new school until she starts kindergarten.

John and I agree: We will use some rental income to pay for June's pre-school. Though the school is one of the most expensive in the area, it also has the lowest ratio of students to teachers. This means that June will get more attention from the teachers than at other schools.

The teachers I met while visiting the school seem genuinely interested in treating the students like they were their own children.

I am sad to be leaving June all day, but she seems to be in good hands. John and I have been reviewing the budget, our income, and respective careers in an attempt to find out how soon one of us could retire from our full-time job and stay at home with June.

So far, it looks like ten years from now. If we find a couple more successful rental properties, this timeline could be significantly shorter.

I just had my annual review. Not only do I receive a substantial raise, I also received a promotion to management. I am now the supervisor for the accounts receivable area. I have three people working for me that only yesterday were my peers.

REFLECT AND PAUSE

"Have no fear of perfection–
you'll never reach it."

- Salvador Dali

I ran to HR to find out more about the management classes advertised in the company newsletter. I told Gayle, in HR, that I was a bit concerned about my new position and she suggested I read a couple of motivational books, like Jim Rohn or Tony Robbins. She also tells me how the management courses I have seen in the newsletter are structured.

She points out that I could take some management classes at the local college and the company would reimburse me 100 percent for any course I maintain an A or B average in, or 75 percent for a C.

At lunch, I make some calls and find out that two of the nearby colleges are currently in open enrollment. I check out the course offerings and find the college nearest to my home is offering an Introduction to Management course on Tuesday and Thursday nights starting in two weeks. I registered for the course.

Wow! Despite juggling a full-time job, new baby, husband and lots of new challenges at work, I earned an 'A' in the Intro to Management course. The company just reimbursed me for the course, and I am reviewing the course curriculum for some upper level management classes.

In reviewing the curriculum I notice there is an Introduction to the Stock Market and Investing class starting soon. I have been thinking that John and I need to diversify our investments and this seems like a good next step.

So I signed up for the stock market class. As the curriculum mentions that topics include budgeting, researching stocks, understanding the broader market and how it affects individual stocks and the global economy, plus identifying stock trends, I checked with Gayle in HR to see if this class would qualify for reimbursement. She says that I would be reimbursed as this class is an option under the management degree program. As the policy has not changed, this means that I will be reimbursed 100 percent for an A or a B, and 75 percent for a C.

I am planning a one-year birthday party for June. It just doesn't seem possible. I have started the stock market class and am learning quite a bit.

The instructor insisted that all students create a paper trading account, whether it is literally on paper or using the Internet. I don't have time to create an internet trading account so I am doing my trading on paper.

He also suggests we get access to the Investors Business Daily (IBD) newspaper. I can get 2-weeks free for the home delivery version or 4-weeks free for the Internet only version of the paper. I decide to get the 4-weeks of internet only access. This gives me an extra 2 weeks to access the information for free and see if this is a resource I want to continue using.

The instructor is showing us how he uses the newspaper, both the local paper and the IBD to find suggestions for stock picks as well as timing of entry and exit to the market.

I go to the library and read some other books on investing to see other authors' opinions on the market. It is interesting to see how various people interpret the same data and come up with vastly differing opinions on what it means and how to use that information to make money.

So far, my paper trading has yielded a 10 percent return on my investment. I can't wait to get started with real money. I also realize that stock investing is riskier than real estate investing, so I will first review the budget and see how much we can afford to risk in the stock market.

My goal is to make money, but I must be realistic and plan as if I could lose all of it. That way, if things go terribly wrong, I won't be in financial difficulty.

I keep thinking back to when I first started in real estate investing. I had my landlords to mentor me and it worked well. So I ask my instructor if he will mentor me or can suggest someone who is a successful stock investor who might agree to mentor me.

My instructor is rather surprised by the question. He says he has been teaching the material for over 15-years and I am the first student to ask him about ongoing support. He feels that, as I am still a student, the relationship could be misconstrued as favoritism. He recommends a former student who had done very well as a stockbroker since graduating from college.

I contact Fred and he graciously agrees to mentor me. He first asks if I have a budget and know how much I am willing to risk on stock trades. I tell him I do and that I also have a trading philosophy. No more than 10 percent invested in any one stock and I will re-evaluate my portfolio once a week on Saturday.

If a stock has reached a sell price, whether that is due to the stock price falling below my stop loss price or rising above my profit price, I will execute a sell order. If there is news on a stock that leads me to believe that the fundamentals have changed and the stock is headed for trouble I will also put in a sell order for that stock, regardless of the price.

Fred agrees that my stock investing philosophy is realistic. He agrees to work with me to increase my knowledge and reach my goals.

So, I add a budget item for stock investing, do the research on the stocks, and make small gains on small amounts invested. As my confidence grows, and I have more money to invest because of my gains, I buy larger blocks of stock. Then I find a stock that returns 1000 percent. It was trading at twenty-five cents a share and is about to be de-listed when I find it.

My mentor isn't sure I should invest in the company until I show him my research. The company makes products that everyone uses every day. They just do a lousy job of marketing themselves.

I also show Fred that the company has cash on hand worth fifty cents per share. This means the company could buy back every outstanding share and still have operating income. I decide it is worth the gamble and buy 5000 shares at twenty-five cents each.

Because I am impressed with the company and its products, I make some phone calls to the company trying to find out who their marketing director is and offer my services to help get the word out about the company and the products.

The marketing director is intrigued by my proposal and offers me stock options in lieu of salary to put my plan in motion. I arrive at an agreement with the marketing director and then call Ken, a friend from college, who works at an ad agency.

I explain my proposal and ask for some insight on how to pull it off. After some haggling Ken agrees to a flat fee based on a percentage increase in the value of my stock options. This means Ken is paid only if I make money.

It also means that Ken will keep me focused and on track so he can get paid.

Ken tells me it takes a long time to get ideas into media print. Local radio stations, on the other hand, often have time to sell and local cable TV stations have public access channels that offer free TV time to anyone. I checked into these options and secured two thirty (30) second radio spots one at 4:30 am and one at 7:30 pm in the next month in Minneapolis/St. Paul market. When I check out the local cable TV station, they agree to give me a spot, but require me to attend a class to learn how to run a cable program, use props, equipment, etc.

Fortunately, there are classes starting immediately. I signed up to attend a class on Thursday nights for five weeks. While taking the class I discovered I really like directing. When I successfully complete the class, the station manager offers me a slot at 10 am on Tuesday a month later.

The radio ad runs while I am working on the cable TV angle and the stock jumps to fifty cents per share. I double my money and people are starting to find out about the company and the products.

With this increase in stock price, I am able to sell some shares of stock and pay Ken for his services. He is so surprised by the quick return on his investment, he decides to buy some shares of the stock. He also offers me some advice on improving the commercials that have already aired.

My mentor is now interested in the company and decides to buy some stock. My instructor is still skeptical. Because my instructor has been investing for a long time, he also knows that sometimes the difference between a successful and unsuccessful company is the marketing.

The company is quite impressed with what I accomplished and is astounded when I mention I'm working on a cable TV infomercial. They liked the radio ads, but asked that they be given final say on the

TV ad. I agree and call Ken in advertising to get insight into creating a TV infomercial.

After our discussion, I decided to use a 15-minute infomercial format. It seems to be more versatile than other choices and works well with the company's product line. Once the infomercial is filmed, I send a copy of the video to the company.

The company is so impressed by the quality of the infomercial, they offer to pay me the going rate for a 15-minute infomercial. I agree, with the stipulation that my name remains in the credits as director anytime the ad is shown.

I reminded the PR person that I had already received stock options for my original suggestions on how to improve their marketing, however he insisted that I should be compensated for the work I did to create the infomercial.

The company takes my infomercial and breaks it into 30 second and 1-minute ads. These ads air during national prime time TV programs. The company also sends the 15-minute infomercial to a number of cable TV stations for rebroadcast.

Since I initially found the stock about 9 months ago, the company has become a household name and the stock is now worth $5.00 per share.

In my weekly review of my stock portfolio, I realize that this stock is a large part of my current net worth. To reduce the amount of my net worth directly attributable to this company, I exercise some of my stock options.

This means that I put in an order to buy the stock at the exercise price and then another order to sell those same shares at the market price. At the end of the day, I have netted $100,000. To avoid tax issues in April, I send a check for $50,000 to the IRS (Internal Revenue Service).

Note: I do this because I am a W-2 employee and want to make sure I do not have to pay a penalty when I file my tax return in April. If I was self-employed and sending in estimated taxes on a quarterly basis, I would check with my tax accountant on how much and when to send it to the IRS.

As much fun as I have had with this stock, I realize I have not had time to research other opportunities. At this point, I decide to review the stocks on my watch list, and see if any of them are viable candidates for trading. If not, I'll go back to the newspaper and the Internet to research new candidates.

Due to the incredible success I had with this one stock, John and I are reviewing our budget to see when one or both of us can retire.

We decide to continue doing what we are doing for the next 5 years and to review the budget annually.

We just learned about a 30-unit condominium style apartment complex and realize we can use the money from the stock sale as a down payment. It's much larger than anything we have bought before. I check with Paul, our real estate agent, and my personal banker about any additional items we need to review when buying commercial property.

Since we don't know much about the building, I decided to drive over to the property and visit the existing tenants. I find the building is somewhat run down, but it appears to be structurally sound. The tenants all say the same thing. They hate the landlord and are looking for ways to break their leases without incurring any penalties. Their two main complaints are lack of hot water, and low water pressure.

I do a little more digging and find out each unit is individually metered for electric and gas service and each unit has its own hot water heater installed in a hall closet. I find a few tenants who say their only complaint is the water pressure, they have no issue with hot water. I also discovered those units have very old water heaters that would probably need to be replaced soon.

PRIORITIZE

"Easy payments, easy lease, easy approval.
Debt is very EASY to get into, but
makes it HARD to live victoriously."

- Bradley Vinson

After crunching some numbers, I decide that putting in a low-ball offer with a contingency for inspection, mortgage approval, and a detailed accounting of all items that convey is an appropriate next step.

The property inspector finds that the low water pressure is caused by an improper connection to the city water lines. He assures me that a couple of phone calls to the city can get the water pressure issue resolved. He even gives me the names of the people to call and what to say to get them to help.

The water heaters, on the other hand, are a much bigger issue. The inspection reveals that service capacity is too small to handle the electrical needs of the newer water heaters. In the building's current state, the new water heaters would never work properly.

At this point, it is time to get an electrician to give me an estimate on what it will cost to bring the building up to code. The electrician came back with an estimate of $10,000 and this was contingent upon him not finding any surprises when he started running the new service throughout the building.

I go back to the seller and tell him about the electrical problems. He acts surprised, and I offer him the following options: Either he can fix the electrical system and provide proof that the building is now up to code without a change to the selling price, or I am reducing the sale price by $10,000 to cover the necessary electrical work.

The owner agrees to reduce the sales price. He has now become a serious "don't wanter." Now that the seller and I have agreed on all the details of the transaction, I bring the offer to my bank to apply for the mortgage. Despite the appraisal value of $100,000 more than the contract price of the property, the bank is concerned about the electrical system.

I agree to a contract with the electrical company and include this as part of the mortgage documentation. The work will begin the same day the documents are signed, and the property is mine.

After closing on the sale, I called the city to get the water pressure problem resolved. Within one week of the closing, all the water heaters are working, the electrical system is up to code, and the water pressure problem is permanently resolved.

I then hold a tenant meeting to introduce John and myself and tell them that we would like to know if there are any remaining issues or concerns they have about the building. I also tell them how the issues with the water pressure and water heaters were resolved.

Finally, I ask each of them to prepare a wish-list of improvements they would like to see in the building or their individual units. I realize the tenants are suspicious, so I offer to hold these meetings every other month (6 times a year) to discuss tenant needs, building maintenance, etc., and to keep things from getting antagonistic.

The tenants agree, and we schedule the next meeting in six weeks. Before we adjourn, I ask for volunteers to join an executive committee. The committee members will be available to the other tenants to do minor repairs in exchange for a rent reduction. It's a temporary assignment and continued participation will be based on tenant feedback.

Of the four volunteers, only two received favorable ratings at the next tenant meeting. Of those two, one gentleman was voted most responsive, and I asked him if he would be interested in the resident manager position.

I explain the job, which includes showing prospective tenants around the complex and minor handyman jobs. In exchange, his rent will be reduced to $200 per month. He agrees and asks if I will let the other gentleman be his backup or maintain his membership in the executive committee, so he can also do odd jobs around the complex.

I agree that the executive committee worked well, and that it will now be a two-member committee and we will post that on the tenant news board.

Successive meetings lead not only to improved management/tenant relations but also a new pride in living in the apartment complex. Over time, flowerbeds come to life. The lawn is mowed and fertilized, junk cars are removed from the parking lot, children begin playing on the swings that have been repainted. After a year of ownership, John and I achieved a complete turnaround in the building and the attitude of the tenants.

While the apartment complex is a good investment, I also have other things going on in my life.

My baby is starting kindergarten. How quickly they grow up!

My real estate investments are adding over $3,700 per month to our income. Most of that income is being put into long-term savings for college for June, and our retirement/financial freedom accounts.

The stock investments are doing well. So far I have earned 15 percent per year on my investments, even when I don't factor in that one stock that earned me 1000 percent return.

INVESTING IS FUNDAMENTAL

"When it comes to compounding,
don't trust your intuition–you have
no idea how powerful it is."

- Manoj Arora,
From the Rat Race to Financial Freedom

I have revisited the budget and have concluded that with five more years at our current incomes, both John and I will be able to retire and concentrate on our investment portfolio and raising June. He is so impressed with my stock investing that he has decided to take some classes.

Between John and I, we have amassed a six-figure stock investing account. We have a duplex, a triplex, and a 30-unit apartment complex that are fully rented, except for the one unit we live in.

We have happy tenants and well-maintained properties with few problems. I have spoken to my personal banker about taking some money out of the triplex to invest in some other properties we are researching. He mentioned the best way to do that was to use a home equity line of credit so that we could borrow the money from the equity in the home and could pay it back over time.

The best thing about the line of credit? We can use it and pay it back any number of times during the first ten years of the loan. After the first ten years, we are no longer able to borrow any more money but we get an additional ten years to pay off the balance.

Life is good.

Today is the day! I put in my resignation six months ago to allow an orderly transition. The accounting department is running like a well-oiled machine since I instituted a few changes in the workflow.

I am sad to be leaving the company where I have worked for over ten years, but am happy about where I am going. I will be home to take care of June, to arrange play dates, and to chaperone class trips.

I was driving June to school yesterday and noticed a couple of For Sale signs on the route to school. I am going to call the phone numbers to get more information. Maybe I'll be buying more real estate later this week.

We have Financial Freedom; enough money in the bank to pay for June's college expenses, rental income to pay for current expenses, and investment income from real estate, stocks and bonds to continue adding to our financial freedom account. It is hard to believe how much my life has changed since I first picked up this book.

I can't wait to see how the rest of my life turns out.

FINAL THOUGHTS

Hey there! I just wanted to say thanks so much for picking up this book. I hope it's helped you feel more confident about managing your finances.

If it has, I'd love it if you could spread the word by sharing it with your friends and family on social media.

If you enjoyed the book and found it helpful, I'd really appreciate hearing from you. Taking a minute to leave a review on Amazon would be amazing (you can find it here: https://amzn.to/3Oo0nTK). Your feedback will help me make this book even better and expand the topics in the series.

Also, I've got some additional resources for you here: https://www.josettemandela.com/freegift4u.

I'm rooting for your future success and I believe in you.

Best Regards,

Josette Mandela

https://josettemandela.com

APPENDIX A

SAMPLE BUDGET

Budget Item	January	February	March	April
Income				
Salary 1	3000	3000	3000	3000
Salary 2	1000	1000	1000	1000
Rental Property 1	1200	1200	1200	1200
Rental Property 2	2000	2000	0	2000
Total income:	7200	7200	5200	7200
Expenses				
Home Mortgage	1500	1500	1500	1500
Mortgage 1 (rental 1)	1000	1000	1000	1000
Mortgage 2 (rental 2)	1700	1700	1700	1700
Electric	150	150	150	150
Water/Sewer	100	100	100	100
Phone - Home	50	50	50	50
Auto—gas	100	100	100	100
Food	300	300	300	300
Cell phone	50	50	50	50
Cable TV	50	50	50	50
Internet	100	100	100	100
Total expenses:	5100	5100	5100	5100
Net (income—expenses)	2100	2100	100	2100

ENVELOPES:

Retirement/ FinancialFreedom—10%	466.62	466.62	22.22	466.62
Long-Term Savings—10%	466.62	466.62	22.22	466.62
Education—10%	466.62	466.62	22.22	466.62
Fun—10%	466.62	466.62	22.22	466.62
Giving—5%	233.52	233.52	11.12	233.52
Total savings:	2100	2100	100	2100

As you can see the top part of the budget shows income and expenses, consider this the necessities envelope. The bottom part of the budget shows the remaining envelopes and their percentages.

The breakdown is based on the assumption that the top part of the budget (NEC) consumes 55 percent of the income while the remaining envelopes split up 45 percent of current income.

When you are just starting out, the necessities may take more than 55 percent of the available income.

Here's a quick reminder on how to find the dollar amounts to put into the non-necessities envelopes or bank accounts.

Example:

The net income is 45 percent of the budget when necessities are 55 percent of the budget. Therefore, 10 percent of the net income equals 10 percent of 45 percent or 10/45 or 0.2222. This is the number that you use to multiply net income by to come up with the dollar amount to put in each of the envelopes that say 10 percent.

In our example above: 2100 * 0.2222 = $466.62

Note: If you choose to tithe—give 10 percent to charity, then necessities is only 50 percent and the net income corresponds to 50 percent and the math would be: 10/50 = 0.20 and all the envelopes/accounts would have the same amount of money. 2100 * 0.2 = $420

In this example I also show how the numbers need to be adjusted when you have a rental vacancy.

In the month of March the numbers change to:

100 * .2222 = $22.22 or 100 * .2 = $20

APPENDIX B

BLANK BUDGET FORM

Income/ Month			
Salary 1			
Salary 2			
Rental Property 1			
Rental Property 2			
Other Income 1			
Total:			

Expenses

Loan 1			
Loan 2			
Taxes			
Bills			
Insurance			

Home Mortgage			
Rental Prop 1 Mort			
Rental Prop 2 Mort.			
Life Insurance			
Power			
Gas			
Phones			
Groceries			
Vehicles			
Entertainment			
Total:			
Envelopes			
10% Education			
10% Long-Term Savings			
10% IRA/ Financial Freedom			
10% Fun			
5% Charity			

APPENDIX C

HOW TO PAY FOR EMERGENCIES

My definition of emergency: Something that must be fixed right now or you will be unable to get to work or a repair to your home that cannot be put off without threatening the value, such as a roof leak. It is not a new dress and purse to match, a trip to Atlantic City, or a weekend getaway.

In the early years, the budget will be tight and there will not be a lot of money available for emergencies. To avoid robbing Peter to pay Paul, or in your case, taking money out of your long-term goals to pay for emergencies, try one of the following suggestions.

The easiest way to pay for an emergency is to use a credit card. Credit cards are easy to get, just be careful not to abuse them. Remember we are using the credit card as a short-term loan to pay for an emergency. It is not to be used for buying things you currently cannot afford.

The trick with credit cards is to apply for one with the lowest interest rate and no annual fee. The reason for this is simple. Paying a fee doesn't get you a higher credit limit, but it does take money out of your pocket. You also want the lowest interest rate as it is likely you will be carrying a balance on this card and want to pay as little as possible in interest.

For those who are unfamiliar with credit cards and interest rates, a short answer is the bank is making you a loan when they approve your credit card application. Because credit card debt is considered riskier than other kinds of loans, the bank charges higher interest rates.

For this reason you must be careful when using credit cards for emergencies. Every month you do not pay off the balance the credit card company charges you interest on the amount that you borrowed. In your statement you will see an item called the average daily balance. You will also notice that the average daily balance does not equal the amount of money you initially charged on the credit card. It usually is more and to determine exactly what that number is you need to read the fine print on the back of your credit card statement.

When you decide to use a credit card to pay for an emergency, you must then add the credit card balance to your budget. You can list it using the minimum payment due each month or some other dollar amount greater than that. I recommend as soon as you use the credit card to pay for something you add the total dollar amount due to your budget.

Credit cards are typically considered unsecured loans. This means that your work history as well as your credit history is sufficient for the bank to accept you as a credit risk. They require no other form of collateral to guarantee you will pay them back.

Some of you, either due to bad credit or no credit history, will be asked for some assurance that your loan will be repaid. This is called a secured loan. This means you must offer the bank something of value, such as a savings account or equity in your home, in exchange for giving you a loan.

The value of using either a secured or unsecured loan for emergencies is to build a credit score.

Note: Credit cards are not the only type of loan that can be used. You can also talk to your bank about borrowing money from them and may find they offer better interest rates than the credit card you were applying for.

An unsecured loan is a loan a bank makes to customers based on their credit history and credit score. For long-time customers, a bank may make an unsecured loan based on their experience with you and not ask you to fill out a loan application. However, the small branch bank where everyone knows everyone in town is getting rarer every day and in all likelihood you will be asked to fill out a loan application.

If you cannot qualify for an unsecured loan, ask the banker about using a secured loan. The only difference in the process for a secured loan is the bank asks you to pledge something of equal value to the loan amount.

If you have been saving for a while, you may have money at the bank you can pledge as collateral for the loan. This way you get the money you need for the emergency without affecting the long-term savings account and you add positive entries to your credit report.

Typically, a bank will loan up to $5,000.00 on an unsecured loan. If they feel you do not meet their requirements for an unsecured loan, they will ask if you have any collateral. Collateral can be your long-term savings account. You would pledge the account as collateral for the loan and the bank would then give you the money you asked for. This also means that if you do not pay the loan back, the bank will take the money in your savings account to pay off the loan.

If the bank has to 'foreclose' on the collateral to pay off the secured loan, they will send letters to the credit bureaus stating this. This will adversely affect your ability to get future loans, including but not limited to credit cards, mortgages, or unsecured bank loans. So only agree to a loan if you are serious about paying it back.

Still another source for cash for emergencies could be the equity in your home. Unless you recently bought the house with less than a 10 percent down payment, you should have enough equity in the property to apply for a home equity line of credit. Keep in mind; this is just another form of secured loan. Unlike the other loans we have discussed, this loan is secured by your home and you could find yourself homeless if you do not repay it.

To prevent this from happening, typically a bank will not approve a new loan that will cause the total of all mortgages on the property to exceed 90 percent of the appraised value. This assures both you and the bank that there is still value in the property even as the loans are being repaid.

From the bank's perspective, they like to receive the interest income, as they are making money on their money and this is money they can loan to other people and make more money. They are not interested in owning real estate as owning real estate just costs them money. From your perspective, the loan is a way to get income from the property without having to sell it. It is a win-win situation when used correctly.

If you qualify for the home equity loan, you can access the equity via a credit card and/or checks. Your bank will tell you which of these options is available to you.

Note: Unlike the other loans we've discussed the interest paid on a home equity loan may be tax deductible. To confirm whether the interest paid on your home equity loan qualifies as a tax deductible expense check with your tax advisor.

Paying back a loan, whether secured or unsecured, on time, will improve your credit history even if you have no credit history up to this point. By increasing the number of positive entries on your credit report you are also improving your chance for qualifying for a competitive interest rate on your mortgage, if owning a home is one of your long-term goals.

Even if you are not thinking about buying a home, having a good credit history can yield better rates when buying a car and even lower rates on your credit cards.

Other options for finding money to pay for an emergency could be family, friends, your church, or other civic organizations you belong to. Some of these other money sources could even come with little or no interest payments or even are outright gifts rather than loans that you have to pay back.

And for those that have a lot of things you may find that selling items you no longer use could generate much needed cash. So don't overlook those old records, second car, artwork, jewelry etc. that you have laying around the house, they could be the answer to your current money troubles.

When that emergency appears, do some brainstorming to come up with all the options available to you and pick the one that makes the most sense for your circumstances.

APPENDIX D

OTHER RESOURCES

These are some of the author's favorites books:

Allen, Robert G. Nothing Down for the 90s. New York: Simon & Schuster, 1990.

Allen, Robert G. Multiple Streams of Income, 2nd edition. New Jersey: John Wiley & Sons, Inc., 2004.

Allen, Robert G. Multiple Streams of Internet Income. New Jersey: John Wiley & Sons, Inc., 2001.

Allen and Hansen, Mark Victor. The One Minute Millionaire. New York: Harmony Books, 2002.

Browne, Harry. Why the best-laid investment plans usually go wrong & how you can find safety and profit in an uncertain world. New York: William Morrow and Company, Inc., 1987.

Bryan, Cameron, and Allen, Catherine. The Artist's Way at Work. New York: William Morrow and Company, Inc., 1998.

Carlson PhD, Richard. Don't Worry, Make Money. New York: Hyperion, 1998.

Covey, Merrill, and Merrill, Rebecca R. First Things First. New York: Simon and Schuster, 1994.

Frank, Milo O. How to get your point across in 30 seconds–or Less. New York: Simon and Schuster, 1986.

Fontana PhD, David. Teach Yourself to Dream A Practical Guide. San Francisco: Chronicle Books, 1997.

Gray PhD, John. Men are from Mars, women are from Venus. New York: Harper Collins, 1992.

Hallman and Rosenbloom, Jerry S., Personal financial Planning, 4th edition.

New York: McGraw-Hill Book Company, 1987.

Harney, Kenneth R., Beating Inflation with Real Estate. New York: Random House, 1979.

Hedrick, Lucy H. Five Days to An Organized Life. New York: Bantam Doubleday Dell Publishing Group, Inc., 1981.

Hill, Napoleon. Think and Grow Rich. California: Wilshire Book Company, 1979.

Nickerson, William, How I turned $1,000 into a million in Real estate in my spare time. New York: Simon and Schuster, 1959.

Pond, Jonathan D., Trying to cut costs? 1001 ways to cut your expenses.

New York: Bantam Doubleday Dell Publishing Group, Inc., 1992.

Roane, Susan, How to work a room. New York: Warner Books, 1988.

Robbins, Anthony. Awaken the Giant within: How to take immediate control of your Mental, Emotional, Physical & Financial Destiny. New York: Simon and Schuster, 1991.

Robbins, Anthony. Unlimited Power: The New Science of Personal Achievement. Nightingale Conant Corp, 1989.

Staff of the Changing Times Magazine. Kiplinger's Buying and Selling A Home. Washington, DC: Kiplinger Books, 1990.

Vian, Leo. Beat the Inefficient Market: Investing in Stocks. 2023

Ziglar, Zig, Ziglar on Selling. New York: Ballantine Books, 1991.

SEMINARS

PERSONAL DEVELOPMENT

Visit https://www.josettemandela.com to find upcoming seminars as well as suggestions for events that you may find useful on your personal journey.

APPENDIX E

GLOSSARY

Appraisal: In real estate this is a document created to show the current market value of the property you are buying. It is relative to other properties in the area that have sold recently. Lending institutions use it to decide how much money to loan you. For rental property the value may be based on the income generated by the property. The income includes rents, coin operated laundry on the premises, vending machines, anything that is available to the tenants where you, the owner, receive cash.

Appreciation: The increase in value of a property over time.

Asset: Something of value. It can be real estate, a savings account, a business, or a stock. This is not an inclusive list.

Bind An Offer: In real estate this is a temporary contract requiring both sides to agree to the terms. Once agreed to it then becomes a contract.

Capital Gains: This is the term used when you sell an asset for more than you paid for it. It is used in stock investing and real estate investing. Capital gains are reported on Schedule D.

Cash Flow: Amount of money generated by a rental property or business after all expenses are paid. This number can be negative. Generally your goal is to buy a piece of property or business and have a positive cash flow. In short your income covers your expenses.

Closing Date: In real estate, this is the date you and the other party(s) to the real estate transaction agree to meet and officially transfer the property.

Collateral: In banking, this term refers to pledging something of value in return for a loan. For example: Your bank asks you to pledge a savings account containing $4,000 to give you a $4,000 secured credit card.

Comparable Sales: In real estate, this is a list of property similar to yours that has sold in your neighborhood in a certain time period usually 1-6 months.

Contingency: In a real estate contract, these are the items that the buyer puts into the contract to ensure their rights are protected. It includes things like, the buyer must be able to secure a mortgage on the property, home inspection must confirm that property is in livable condition, all blinds and curtains are to convey, etc.

Contract: A legal document between two parties specifying the terms and conditions each side must perform. In a real estate contract, the seller agrees to sell their property to the buyer for a given sales price on a certain day. The buyer agrees to buy the house for that price on that day assuming all contingencies specified in the contract are met.

Credit Report: This is a historical listing of all your debt and how well you paid it back. There are 3 main credit bureaus that maintain credit histories on you. They are Experian, Equifax, and TRW. They receive their information from the various lending institutions, such as banks or car dealers, who you have used to make purchases. The report includes how much you borrowed, if you paid it back, and how many times you were late.

Credit Score: Also known as FICO score. This is a number that lending institutions use to judge your creditworthiness. It takes into account how much debt you have outstanding, how often you are late paying your bills and affects your ability to get more loans as well as the interest rate you are charged on those loans.

Compounding: Interest is paid on both the principal and accumulated interest from previous time periods. This is distinguished from simple interest (see below).

Delisted: This is a term used for a stock that no longer meets the large stock exchanges criteria to be listed on that exchange. For example, the New York Stock Exchange (NYSE) will delist a stock if its stock price falls below $1.00.

Down Payment: Money a buyer gives to the seller or real estate agent in consideration of an offer to buy their property. This money will be returned to the buyer if all contingencies are not fulfilled. However, if the buyer defaults on the purchase the seller retains the down payment.

Equity: In real estate, the value of a property which exceeds the total amount owed on the property.

Escrow: Money held by a third party that is not turned over until all contingencies have been satisfied. It also refers to money that your mortgage company collects to pay for home owners insurance and taxes, which the bank pays when due.

Exercise Price: This is a term used with stock options. Also known as strike price is a predetermined price at which an option contract can be completed. It is the price that the option holder has a right, but not the obligation to buy (call option) or sell (put option) the underlying stock.

Grandfather Clause: In real estate, this refers to a provision to allow a certain type of development to occur on the property that the law used to allow but now no longer allows.

Gross Income: For an employee of a company this refers to your annual salary. For tax purposes in the United States, it refers to all income earned regardless of its source.

Infomercial: This is a combination of two words: information and commercial.It is usually 15-30minutes long and designed to tell you about a product or service. After describing the product's features and benefits, the infomercial ends with an offer to buy the item or sign up for the service.

Lease: An agreement transferring the right to exclusive possession and use of a particular property to an individual or individuals for a distinct period and a specified fee.

Liability: A thing for which someone is responsible for, especially a debt or financial obligation. This is any loan, credit card balance, etc. that you owe to someone else.

Lien: A claim on the property of another as security for a debt or financial obligation.

Market Value: The price a property might command if offered for sale at that point in time.

Mortgage: This is a loan secured by real estate.

Net income: This is gross income minus deductions, such as taxes paid and 401k contributions, and yields your tax home pay.

Net Worth: This is calculated by subtracting all of your liabilities from all of your assets. This number can be negative.

Profit: Yield or financial gain; to make money on a transaction.

Real Estate Agent: Someone licensed to sell real estate.

Return on investment (ROI): It is a metric used by investors to evaluate profitability of the investment. The amount of profit received on an investment is generally expressed as a percentage. An example: 10 percent ROI is earning $10 on a $100 investment.

Secured Loan: Means a borrower has pledged collateral to receive the loan. Should the borrower default on the loan, the lending institution keeps the collateral as payment.

Security deposit: Money deposited with a landlord by a tenant held for the duration of a lease to cover failure to pay rent or necessary repairs to bring the property back to rentable condition. Also, can be used to compensate for damages caused by the tenant who wrongfully quits the unit prior to the expiration of the lease.

Simple Interest: This means interest is paid on the principal amount only.

Stock Options: These give the holder the right but not the obligation to buy shares of stock at a set price within a certain time frame. It also spells out how many shares can be acquired at that price.

Stop Loss: This is a term used in stock investing. It means an order to sell a stock at a certain price. It is used when the price of the stock could fall and you are trying to limit the amount of money you lose on the transaction.

Unsecured Loan: The borrower acquired the loan based on credit history and credit score alone. With this type of loan no collateral is required. Most credit cards fall in this category.

Watch List: This term is used in stock investing for a list of stocks that you are following. You have done research, like the company, and have decided to invest when certain criteria are met. While waiting you put the stock on a watch list.

ABOUT THE AUTHOR

Josette Mandela is a financial resilience expert and Amazon best-selling author who has a passion for teaching and inspiring women who are struggling with financial overwhelm. She overcame a post-divorce bankruptcy to become a beacon of financial independence.

Her bold philosophy, "A man is not a plan," drives her mission to help women seize control of their financial futures. Combining professional expertise with personal triumph, Josette provides actionable strategies that break down complex financial concepts, inspiring women to build wealth, reclaim their power, and unlock their full potential.

Josette Mandela is currently working on several new projects.

You can connect with Josette online at:

Website: https://www.josettemandela.com

Facebook: https://facebook.com/josettemandela

Amazon Books: amazon.com/author/josettemandela

LinkedIn: https://www.linkedin.com/in/josette-mandela-linked/

Made in United States
North Haven, CT
16 January 2026

86708975R00095